Also by Anne Marie Herman, Author

Protect the Brain with Meningioma Surgery, Memoir

Anne Marie's Family Favorite Recipes with a Caribbean Twist 2018 – Second Edition

Positive Affirmation – Fear No More Memoir
Some Suggestions to Reverse Type 2 Diabetes 2020
First Edition

  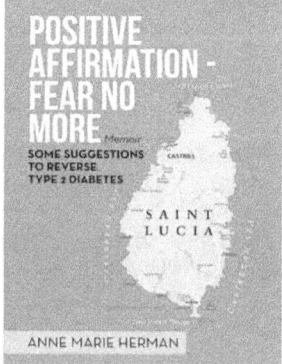

PROTECT THE BRAIN
WITH MENINGIOMA SURGERY

MEMOIR

ANNE MARIE HERMAN

Protect the Brain with Meningioma Surgery
Memoir

Copyright © 2020 by Anne Marie Herman.

Paperback ISBN: 978-1-952982-56-9
Ebook ISBN: 978-1-952982-57-6

All rights reserved. No part in this book may be produced and transmitted in any form or by any means, electronic, or mechanical, including photocopying, recording, or by any information storage and retrieval system, without permission in writing from the copyright owner.

The views expressed in this work are solely those of the author and do not necessarily reflect the views of the publisher hereby disclaims any responsibility for them.

Published by Green Sage Agency 11/16/2020

Green Sage Agency
1-888-366-9989
inquiry@greensageagency.com

ACKNOWLEDGMENT AND APPRECIATION

Author:	Anne Marie Herman, Retired State and University Worker
Style and Format	Aaron Herman, Provided Assistance with Formatting
Proof Reader Assistant	Barb Booth, Made Suggestions
Proofing & Assembling	Joseph Herman, Made Suggestions
Consultants	Valerie and Valendice Payne Provided Opinion on Structure and Format

First Book also written by Anne Marie Herman Cookbook Anne Marie's Family Favorite with a Caribbean Twist Second Edition A cookbook with an array of delicious recipes containing 368 pages. Starting with Appetizers, Bars, Breads, Cakes, cookies, Desserts, Dis and Dat, Drinks, Main Dishes, Meat and Poultry, Pies, Tarts, Side Dishes Pastries, Punch, Salads, Seafoods, Side Dishes, Soups, Vegetables.

Common Substitutions, Math lessons in the Kitchen with kids, Roasting Charts, Commonly used Measurements, and Equivalents, How to Soften Rock Hard White Sugar from Supermarket, Beef Patties, Avocado Dips, Bruschetta with tomato adults love those if they are watching their weight, Eggplant Fritters, Fried Green or Ripe Plantains, Hot Bakes with Cocoa Tea, Roll-Ups, Salt Fish Cakes from the Caribbean, Spinach and Feta Fold-over, Cereal Breakfast Bars, Cream Cheese Pumpkin Bars my granddaughter's favorite, my grand-kids love those, Chocolate Chip Popcorn bars, Favorite Brownies, Mud Hen Bars, Aloha Friendship Bread my church love those, Banana Bread, Bran Muffins, Caribbean Seafood Stew, Citrus glazed Salmon, Baked Green Bananas, Bean Pot Dinner, Broccoli and Ham Quiche, Cheesy Margarita Pizza, Collard Greens, Eggplant & Tomato Parmesan, Flour Dumplings my grand-kids love those, Shrimp Risotto

Second Book: Positive Affirmation Fear No More Memoir –
Some Suggestions to Reverse Type 2 Diabetes
Losing brothers from Heart Attacks,
Family Issues with Heart Disease
Steps to Reverse Diabetes, Food and Insulin, Symptoms of Diabetes, A1C Test Taken, Risk involved, doctor warning, Things you have to know, when am I going back to the Gym, Aerobic Activity, Care for Your Diabetes, Decrease the Amount of food, Carbohydrate Foods, High Fiber Foods, Overeating Difficulties
Duration of Eating Plans, What Foods a
Person with Diabetes can't eat,
How much sleep you need, Medical Terms?

Dear Reader,

After many years of working, I am finally home. It's a strange word, home.

Even though I haven't set my foot on the island of St. Lucia, West Indies for many years, I still remember the warm weather, blue waters, the family, mangoes, and breadfruit the most.

I guess in the back of my mind, I have to see the place again. I am capable of putting my thoughts together. I have spent years writing my book, weeks of researching literary agents, and days crafting the perfect pitch, waiting on a response from an agent, I would like you to give my book another look.

Writing on a computer is a gift from God, and reminds me of what I have done all my life. Example, transcribing dictation, proofing other people's work, creating books for state departments, setting slide presentations and today, I have been writing about my life and accomplishments. Keep in mind I am a domestic goddess who does not like to sit around doing nothing, or just idling. So, I am sharing my findings of my surgeries with you today.

Anne Marie

TABLE OF CONTENTS

Meningioma Brain Tumor Memoir 1
Radiology screening questions 3
What is an MRI? 6
What Does MRI do Exactly? 7
What Problems May be Uncovered by an MRI of the Head and Neck? 8
Why May I be Unable to have an MRI of the Head and Neck? 9
What are the Risks of Having an MRI? 10
Definition of Meningioma 11
What Causes a Meningioma Tumor? 12
Treatments 13
Can Meningioma Cause a Sudden Death? 15
Are Benign Brain Tumors Hereditary? 16
Where Can I find Support for Myself or a Family Member Diagnosed with a Meningioma? 17
Precautions and Contradictions 23
How should I care for My Wound? 24
Going Home and Medicine Plan 25
Reset Your Body 27
Indications for Procedure 28
Details of Procedure 28
Comparison: CT Head Exams dated 8/30/2017 Findings 30

Blunt the effect of SALT in your body 30
Which Foods are Rich in Potassium? 32
What are the causes of low Potassium? 33
What is the Treatment for Low Potassium? Is it Dangerous? 34
What Does Potassium do to your Body? 35
What Foods are Good to Lower Potassium? 36
What are the Warning Signs of Low Potassium? 37
Potassium Amount for the Elderly 39
Sources of Potassium 39
BLUNT the effect of Iron and Fiber 42
How Your Body Uses Iron in Food 43
How to Get More Iron from Your Food 45
Food Selection for Diabetes 45
Going Home 45
Author's Shunt Surgery with Hydrocephalus 47
Why does Hydrocephalus Occur? 48
How is Hydrocephalus Treated? 49
How Can Parents Help 49
Definition of Hydrocephalus 50

What is a Shunt? 52
What are the Side Effects of a Shunt Placement? 53
What is the Life Expectancy for Hydrocephalus Spine & Spinal Nerve? 53
Ways to Live Longer 53
Get Married 55
Ways to Stay Healthy 56
Men Don't Like to Talk 57
My Struggle to Overcome Lifelong Fear of Swimming Coming from an Island 57

Husband Teaching Wife How to Drive a Stick Shift 59
Boy Scout White Water Rafting High Adventure Trip 60
Someone Lost a Tooth on the Playground While Playing
Scatter Dodgeball in Grade School 61
My Oldest Brother's Plight 62
Bibliography 65
Medical Terms Glossary 67
Acknowledgments And Appreciation 75
About the Author 79
Protect the Brain with Meningioma Surgery Memoir 79
First Edition 79

PREFACE

MENINGIOMA BRAIN TUMOR MEMOIR

The purpose of this memoir is to outline how a medical examination performed using Magnetic Resonance Imaging (MRI) discovered a benign meningioma tumor in this author's head three years ago. After looking at the MRI, the doctors concluded that she needed surgery.

According to the neurosurgeon's note, imaging and MRI of the patient's brain with and without contrast on January 23, 2017 was personally viewed and was reviewed with the patient. This MRI was significant for 5.6X3.9X4cm extra axil dual based mass which exerts local mass effect on the frontal lobe, frontal horns bilaterally, right greater than left, and basal ganglia with mild associated vasogenic edema.

CT scan of the neck from January 13, 2017 was also viewed which did not show a discrete lipoma or soft tissue mass. There are two enhancing soft tissue lesions within the visualized intracranial contents.

Assessment Plan: Patient was referred to neurological surgeon for two masses that were visualized on her MRI which are most compatible with meningiomas. A second mass was located in the fossa. Doctor recommended surgery for this patient. Will require two craniotomy surgeries to remove these masses. Doctor would like to perform surgery to remove the right frontal lobe mass. Want to make a trans coronal incision with a primary approach as well as a low frontal approach above the air sinuses to get more medial to the mass.

Patient had poor understanding and insight into her condition which she likely had from the tumor as it was located in the frontal lobe. Advised the patient that neurosurgeon would like to meet with her again to further discuss these surgeries with her. She did report that her children might be able to come with her to the appointment. Neurosurgeon also advised patient to stop taking aspirin, ibuprofen, or Aleve as this can increase the risk of bleeding into these masses.

On July 11, 2017, this author was admitted at the UW Hospital and Clinics till the 19 of July for craniotomy. Just before she was admitted at the hospital, she was blessed by a catholic priest, Father Tafadzwa Kushamba, who had recently been ordained at St. Maria Goretti church as a Parochial Vicar priest. At that time, she was afraid and not aware of what would happen to her, nor telling the priest she was going for major surgery to pray for her. Later on, she discovered one of the churchgoers mentioned while they were saying the rosary in church, that the author was going to have major surgery and to pray for her. She was sent several get-well cards and prayers at home while she was at the hospital. The church sent visitors and representatives to the hospital to visit her and prayed with her when she was feeling better.

The author's sister Helena and brother Denis called so many times checking on her, and it seems her brother Denis was losing his composure as he was touched by the author's condition. The sister and her churchgoers prayed in church for the author. Her nephew Harry in California called to check several times. Her cousin Lucille in Milwaukee called and visited with her children while the author was in rehab later. This surgery was for a craniotomy.

In September 2017, the author was readmitted at the UW Hospital again for placement of a shunt which is still in her head today.

On September 14th through September 20th this author was in rehab for nursing care treatment after surgery and was sent back to rehab for low potassium. As you can see, she was not eating enough ripe bananas to get enough potassium as it is a vital to the health functioning of all human body's cells, tissues, and organs. It also helps to control the amount of water in your body and to maintain a healthy blood PH level. She learned how to take better care of herself at the hospital after she was discharged.

How did the author survive this major surgery? That was a miracle by itself as the author prayed day and night from a little prayer book that was sent to her by her sister. The night before surgery, she prayed with her son and husband asking god for help and assistance in handling her condition. Now she is working on her third book since the operation.

Diagnosis = Brain Tumor. Individualized A1C goal. Reason other comorbidities less than 7.5. Notes attending addendum by neurosurgeon – I saw and evaluated the patient, discussed and agree with the resident's findings and plan. See resident's note that follow.

Author is a mature female here today for new patient evaluation with a large meningioma January 30, 2017.

RADIOLOGY SCREENING QUESTIONS

- Can patient be given oral contrast? Yes.
- Is patient allergic to IV contrast Iodine? No.
- Does patient require a creatine level; must be obtained within the last month for patient's matching the following (select all applicable or none) diabetic treated within insulin or other provider prescribed medication and over 60? No
- Does patient have a pacemaker or defibrillator? No.
- Relevant Surgical History? Eye surgery or eye implant? Yes.
- Implant Devices? None.
- History of metal in body? None.
- If so what type of sedation is needed? None

Neurosurgeon wrote to doctors on his finding's frontal lobe with mass effect on the bilateral frontal lobes and mild associated vasogenic edema. The second mass was located in the fossa.

Neurosurgeon claims author denies any headaches, any focal weakness in arms or legs, any visual speech changes or any numbness or tingling in arms or legs. She reports not having difficulty with memory or any neurological symptoms. Evaluated by primary care and it was felt that this was a lipoma.

On February 23, 2017, this author was hospitalized for the resection of large meningiomas and was started on dexamethasone taper which produced hyperglycemia currently controlled. Since her doses of dexamethasone have been decreased, an IV insulin and continue the regimen. Medicine was ordered to correct for possible hyperglycemia. Doctors anticipate that as her dexamethasone doses are decreased her insulin needs will gradually decrease. Case was discussed with staff attending.

Following the surgical procedure, she was started on high dose steroids and was subsequently noted to have big readings. This prompted the initiation of an IV insulin. A medical consultant was then requested for assistance with the inpatient management of her diabetes management.

Following her surgery her appetite was variable. She had intermittent headaches and pressure at the sight of the surgical incisions.

If her insulin rate was still elevated, doctors would likely decrease the dose of metformin given to her. If the insulin rates were still elevated on February 23, 2017, doctors would likely start prandial insulin administration to insulin her off insulin. A learning center consultation would be called in case she needed insulin at the time of her discharge.

Neurosurgeon noted "I saw and evaluated patient 2/25/17. I have reviewed the note from the endocrine fellow and agree with the finding's assessment plan. The patient had uncontrollable type 2 diabetes, should be resection of meningioma on steroids post-op.

Has been managed on an insulin drip. Her steroids were being tapered. Agree with plan as detailed above".

Patient was first referred for two dual masses which were mostly meningioma and was greater than 5 centimeter and located in the right frontal lobe with mass effect on the bilateral frontal lobe and mild associated vasogenic edema.

The second mass was located in the posterior fossa superior to the foramen magnum and was smaller in size and is not causing any compression to the brainstem at the time.

The lesion was first discovered when she had a persistent noddle in the posterior cervical area of her neck, which was chronic and unchanged which prompted scans, which subsequently found the meningiomas. She denies headaches, focal weakness in her arms and legs, any visual or speech changes, or any numbness or tingling in her arms and legs. She did report that was possibly having more difficulty with memory. Otherwise, she denies any neurological symptoms.

Patient was agreeable to participate in the therapy sessions. RN cleared patient for participation in therapy. No family members were present.

Patient's medical condition was appropriate for Speech Language Therapy intervention. Observation of patient Vital signs: Patient was seated in bedside chair in Neuro ICU.

Patient engaged in interview, formal, and informal evaluation tasks as documented. Effort was good throughout evaluation. PT demonstrated a broad affect and was pleasant and cooperative throughout. Patient was able to state events from hospitalization as well as doctor's plan with mild difficulty.

Patient with moderate difficulty maintaining attention during session, requiring frequent redirection. She was tangential and distracted by environmental stimuli.

Patient was able to recall biographical and social information, however, demonstrates min-mod difficulty during more structured tasks. Patient at times perseverative on topics.

Patient intermittently impulsive throughout session. Patient with slowness of processing speed and reduced cognitive endurance at the time reporting increased headache and fatigue over course session.

Patient with difficulty during sequencing and planning tasks. As patient was highly independent at baseline, recommend ongoing assessment of functional cognitive-linguistic skills.

WHAT IS AN MRI?

A magnetic resonance imaging scan is also called an MRI. An MRI uses magnetic fields and radio waves to take pictures of the inside of your body. This test helps caregivers see normal and abnormal areas of the brain. An MRI can show how and where blood is flowing in our brain. It can also help caregivers see how our brain is working.

An MRI can see tissues, bones, blood vessel, and joints in your head, neck, and spine. Joints are where bones meet. An MRI also shows your inner ears, orbits (eye sockets), sinuses, thyroid gland, and mouth.

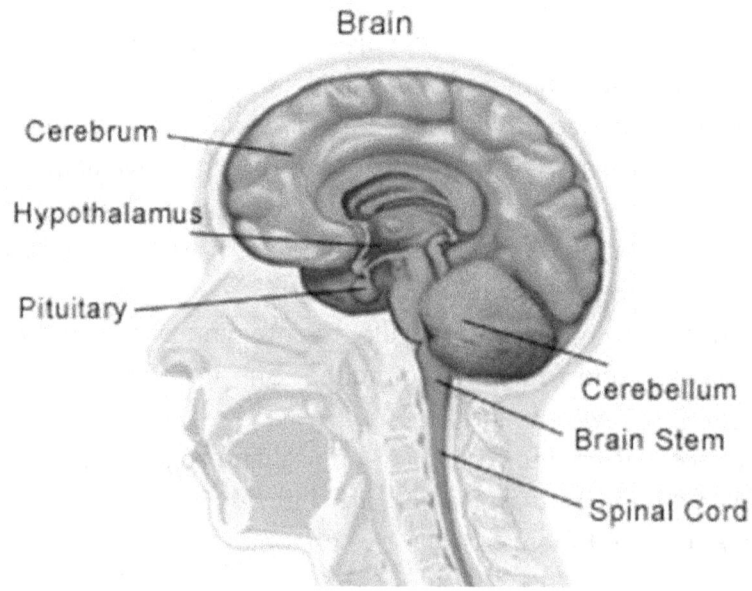

WHAT DOES MRI DO EXACTLY?

MRI of the body uses a powerful magnetic field, radio waves and a computer to produce detailed pictures of the inside of your body. It may be used to help diagnose or monitor treatment for a variety of conditions within the chest, abdomen and pelvis. MRI was used to safely monitor a tumor.

WHY DO I NEED AN MRI OF THE HEAD AND NECK?

You may need an MRI for any of the following reasons:

- You are having symptoms including headaches, dizziness, or memory loss. An MRI may help caregivers learn what is causing your symptoms.
- An MRI can guide or help caregivers plan procedures, such as brain surgery or a biopsy. This is when a sample of tissue is collected from a body area. Functional MRI which maps out areas of the brain, may be done before brain surgery.
- If you are being treated for a disease, an MRI may show how well your treatment is working. It can also check if a disease that you have already been treated for has returned.
- If you have a disease condition that needs treatment, the results of an MRI can help you and your caregiver decide on the best options for you.
- You need a medical device placed in your brain. An MRI may also be used during the surgery to insert the device. Medical devices include those used to decrease the movement problems caused by diseases.
- An MRI may be done after a procedure to look for bleeding and other problems.
- An MRI can check for diseases, such as Alzheimer disease.

WHAT PROBLEMS MAY BE UNCOVERED BY AN MRI OF THE HEAD AND NECK?

- You may need an MRI to help diagnose the following medical conditions:
- Blood vessel problems: An MRI can show widened, narrow, or blocked blood vessels in the head or neck. It may show abnormal growth of blood vessels.
- Growths, such as a mass or tumor: An MRI can show growth in one or more areas of the head or neck. This may include a growth on the lip or tongue, or in the nose or sinuses (air cavities in the bones of the face). A growth may be found in or on the thyroid gland or the brain. The MRI may show a growth in the eye socket or the ear. An MRI can show a growth has spread to the lymph nodes or other parts of the body. Lymph nodes are small organs in the body that fight off the germs that may cause infection.
- Infection: An MRI may show an infection in the inner ear, sinus, or eye socket.
- Stroke or brain damage: A stroke can happen if blood clot prevents blood from getting to certain parts of the brain. When blood cannot reach an area of the brain, tissue may die. Brain damage can happen after a stroke or following trauma (a head injury). An MRI of the head shows the presence and extent of damage of the brain. It may also help caregivers predict recovery in a person who has had brain damage or who is unconscious.
- Dementia is a disease that may occur with older age, causing problems with memory, speech, and movement. An MRI can show areas of the brain that have signs of dementia.
- Epilepsy is a condition that causes seizures (body movements that cannot be controlled). An MRI shows areas of blood flow in the brain and may help caregivers plan epilepsy surgery, if needed.

WHY MAY I BE UNABLE TO HAVE AN MRI OF THE HEAD AND NECK?

Before having an MRI, tell caregivers if any of the following are true for you:

- Are you pregnant? Your caregiver may not want you to have an MRI during your pregnancy, unless it is an emergency.
- Are you allergic to iodine or dye? Dye (contrast liquid) may be used during an MRI. If you know that you are allergic to iodine (found in shellfish, such as shrimp) or dye, tell your caregiver.
- You have metal in your body: This includes insulin pump or a prosthetic (manmade) body part. It also includes screws and plates that may have been placed during surgery.
- You have medical device in your body that contains metal.
- You have claustrophobic fear of small, closed spaces. If you have this fear, caregivers may offer you medicine to help you relax or go to sleep during the MRI.
- You have trouble lying flat or still? You may have a medical condition that makes it very hard to lie flat or without moving for a period of time.

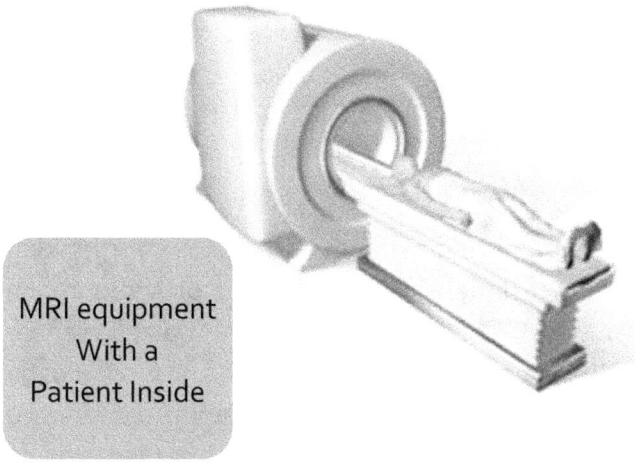

MRI equipment With a Patient Inside

WHAT WILL HAPPEN DURING AN MRI OF THE HEAD AND NECK

- You will be asked to remove any jewelry, and all removable metal objects. If you have a medical device, it may need to be turned off before your MRI. You will lie down on a table with your arms at your sides or over your head. Your caregiver may put padding cushion around and under you. You will need to hold very still during the test so the pictures are clear.

WHAT ARE THE RISKS OF HAVING AN MRI?

- If dye is used during the MRI, it may damage your kidneys. This risk is higher if you have diabetes or kidney disease. If you have metal in or on your body during the MRI, the metal may heat to dangerous level and cause burn. If you had surgery to have a coil, stent, or filter placed in your body recently, it may move out of place during the MRI. This author has her shunt adjusted in her head each time she has the MRI test in July. They always ask her not to leave after the MRI as the adjustment has to be made first as the MRI machine moved the shunt during the test.

WHAT IS THE DIFFERENCE BETWEEN MRI AND AN X-RAY?

X-ray is the well-established technique that allows for looking inside the body in two dimensions, while MRI provides much more comprehensive test. There are some substantial differences between MRI scanning and X-ray scanning. MRI is more costly than X-rays. While MRI and X-ray are both imaging techniques for organs of the body, the difference is that MRI images provide a 3D representation of organs, which X-rays usually cannot. MRI allows for quality scanning and helps in solving a range of medical problems.

With X-rays, the body is exposed to dangerous ionizing radiation, while MRI doesn't emit ionizing. MRI is preferable for soft tissues evaluation while X-rays are preferable for bones.

WHAT DOES MENINGIOMA MEAN?

A meningioma is a tumor that arises from the meninges – the membranes that surround your brain and spinal cord. Although this is not technically a brain tumor, it is included in this category because it may compress or squeeze the adjacent brain, nerves and vessels. Meningioma is the most common type of tumor that forms in the head. Most meningiomas grow very slowly, often over many years without causing any symptoms.

MENINGIOMA DEFINITION IN MEDICAL DICTIONARY

A tumor of meninges and meningeal cells, which is most common in middle-aged women and may occur in a background of neurofibromatosis type 2. Aggressive meningiomas are characterized by bone destruction, florid mitotic activity and metastases. Clinical findings.

Meningioma – Symptoms and causes:
There are no symptoms – according to the Mayo Clinic
See all results for this question
How is a meningioma diagnosed?

DEFINITION OF MENINGIOMA

A common type of slow-growing, usually benign brain tumor that arise from the dura, one of the meninges, the membranes covering the brain and spinal cord. A meningioma may occur wherever there is dura (the outermost of the three meninges), but the most common sites are over the cerebral hemispheres of the brain.

To diagnose a meningioma, a neurologist will conduct a thorough neurological exam followed by an imaging test, such as: Computerized Tomography (CT) scan. CT scans take X-rays that create cross-sectional images of a full picture of your brain. Sometimes an iodine-based dye is used to augment the picture.

WHAT IS THE PROGNOSIS FOR SOMEONE WITH MENINGIOMA?

Better outcomes are associated with a surgical removal of the entire tumor or radiosurgery. The younger the patient is at time of diagnosis, the better the long-term prognosis.

WHAT CAUSES A MENINGIOMA TUMOR?

These mutated cells create copies of themselves, which can slowly accumulate into a tumor. Researchers have discovered several meningioma causes that can trigger these cellular changes, including: Genetic mutations – Up to 80 percent of all meningiomas contain an abnormality on Chromosome 22.

Meningioma definition is – a slow-growing encapsulated typically benign tumor arising from the meninges and often causing damage by pressing upon the brain and adjacent parts.

MENINGIOMA DEFINITION IN THE CAMBRIDGE ENGLISH DICTIONARY

A brain tumor that grows from the meninges (=the three layers of tissue) that surround the brain.

MENINGIOMA BRAIN TUMOR – MEDICAL CONDITION

Tumor that originates from the protective covering of the brain.

A condition in which a (usually) non-cancerous tumor develops from the membrane that surround the brain and spinal cord.

Can last several years or be lifelong – Its cause is not yet found, but is assumed that it occurs due to some cell disorder. It is usually lacking obvious signs, but as it grows, the patient experiences headache, change in vision, hearing disability and ringing in ears. It requires immediate medical attention, or can last for lifetime. The available treatment options include surgery or therapies like stereotactic radiosurgery or fractioned stereotactic radiotherapy.

Symptoms – Meningioma brain tumor usually comes with no symptoms, as it grows gradually the patient may show the following symptoms:

- Headache Which Gets Severe With Time
- Change In Vision Causing Double Or Blurred Vision
- Loss Of Memory And Difficulty In Concentrating
- Weakness In Arms And Legs
- Loss Of Smell
- Seizures
- Numbness
- Speech Problems

TREATMENTS

Treatment depends upon the size and rate of growth of the tumor, age, and overall health issues. Medical procedures: Craniotomy: Stereotactic radiosurgery. Fractioned stereotactic radiotherapy, intensity modulated radiation therapy, Proton beam radiation.

CAUSES

Possible causes of the condition are as follows:

- Alteration or disorder of cells in meninges leading to the formation of tumor
- Exposure to radiations due to radiation therapy or any other factor
- Genetic Disorder like Neurofibromatosis Type 2
- High Body Mass Index or Obesity
- Family history
- Injury or fracture in skull

Most meningiomas occur in the brain. But they can also grow on parts of the spinal cord. Often, meningiomas cause no symptoms and require no immediate treatment. But the growth of benign meningiomas can cause serious problems. In some cases, such growth can be fatal.

The spinal cord serves as an information pathway between your brain and the peripheral nerves that serve the rest of your body. It's quite delicate and requires a lot of protection. Your spinal cord has three coverings and is sheltered in the vertebral column.

MENINGIOMA BRAIN TUMORS

They can grow to a large size prior to being diagnosed because of loss of sense of smell, altered personally or changes in mental status. Wing meningiomas: grow at the base of the skull on either side. The tumors can cause bulging of the eye, visual problems, altered sensation in the face, or seizures.

CAN MENINGIOMA CAUSE A SUDDEN DEATH?

Meningioma is a common intracranial tumor and it is rarely associated with sudden, unexpected deaths. Case report: This author was diagnosed with meningioma in 2017 and the UW Health neurosurgeons and a team of doctors worked tirelessly about 7 hours to remove the tumor and she is doing fine today.

CAN A MENINGIOMA CAUSE DEATH?

Patients with advanced grades of meningiomas are more likely to have a recurrence of the meningioma after treatment and are more likely to have a higher risk of death overall. The five-year recurrence-free survival in grade II meningioma has been described at 87 percent compared to 29 percent for grade III.

WHAT BRAIN TUMOR CAUSES DEATH?

According to research on June 5, 2015, benign meningiomas arising from the meninges (membranes surrounding our brains) often are asymptomatic, but can cause e.g. seizures, they usually grow very slowly. If no (surgical) decompression is possible, rapidly expanding mostly malignant tumors in the brain could cause death by raising the intracranial pressure above a critical threshold.

CAN YOU SURVIVE A BRAIN TUMOR?

Originally Answered: Can you survive a brain tumor? Brain Tumor – the brain consists of cells that divide, grow, die, and new cells are created and sometimes in these cases as an individual may experience abnormal growth of cells in the brain which forms a lump or mass.

ARE BENIGN BRAIN TUMORS HEREDITARY?

Research on May 10, 2017 – A risk factor is anything that increase a person's chance of developing a brain tumor. Although risk factors often influence the development of a brain tumor, most do not directly cause a brain tumor. Some people with several risk factors never develop a brain tumor, while others with no known risk factors do.

ARE BRAIN TUMORS AND BRAIN CANCER THE SAME?

Research on July 16, 2019. Cancer is a term reserved for malignant tumors. Malignant tumors can grow and spread aggressively, overpowering healthy cells by taking their space, blood, and nutrients. Malignant primary brain tumors are cancers that originate in the brain, typically grow faster than benign tumors, and aggressively invade surrounding tissue.

WHAT ARE THE SYMPTOMS OF END STAGE BRAIN CANCER?

It can cause the pressure inside the brain to rise. This can cause headaches, vomiting and mental changes. The immediate site of where the tumor is, determines what neurological problems are the result.

MENINGIOMAS: FIVE THINGS YOU SHOULD KNOW

Most meningiomas (90 percent) are categorized as benign tumors, with the remaining 10 percent being a typical or malignant. In many cases, benign meningiomas grow slowly. This means that depending upon where it is located, a meningioma may reach a relatively large size before it causes symptoms.

WHAT ARE THE RISK FACTORS OF MENINGIOMAS?

Meningiomas are most common in people between the ages of 40 and 70, and are more common in women than in men. Meningiomas are very rare in children.

HOW SUCCESSFUL IS MENINGIOMA TREATMENT?

There are generally three treatment options for meningiomas:

- Observation – If a meningioma is small and asymptotic in a person over 65, it may just be observed. Observation requires annual CT or MRI scans with contrast. Can also be observed for a period of 3 to 12 months before a definitive treatment decision is made.
- Surgery is the primary treatment for meningioma.
- Radiotherapy – Several recent studies have shown radiotherapy to control tumor growth by age 50. If a meningioma is benign and in a part of the brain where neurosurgeons can safely completely remove it, surgery is likely to be the only treatment needed.

Eighty percent of patients reported satisfaction with the quality of their lives after undergoing treatment.

WHERE CAN I FIND SUPPORT FOR MYSELF OR A FAMILY MEMBER DIAGNOSED WITH A MENINGIOMA?

According to research, your physician can answer questions about meningioma diagnosis and help you select appropriate treatment options. Several treatment options are available for meningiomas, chosen based on several factors including the size of the tumor, its location, whether the tumor is causing any symptoms in the patient or not, age, and overall health of the patient. In some cases, more than one treatment option may be used, not only when the tumor is first treated, but also over time should the tumor progress and reoccur.

In deciding the particular course of treatment for a patient, the benefits of each treatment option or combination of treatment options are weighed against the associated risks. It should also be noted that sometimes there is not an obvious "right" choice, because how effective a particular option is may not be fully understood. As newer treatment possibilities emerge and studies are done to look at how successful various options and combination of options are, the recommended course of treatment for patients will continue to evolve.

Prior to surgery, neuroimaging (primarily MRI) of the tumor is performed to help in the planning of the surgical approach to be taken and can also be used during surgery providing 3-dimentional guided imagery. While the location of the tumor will influence the particular surgical approach chosen, most often a neurosurgeon will remove a piece of skull bone to gain access to the brain. In my case the blood supply was cut or stopped to get access to the brain. This operation is called a craniotomy. After surgery, the bone is usually put back in place and secured with small plates and screws. Sometimes due to complications, the bone cannot be replaced, or replaced immediately, in which case other materials are used to cover the hole in the skull and protect the brain. As pointed out previously, complete removal of the tumor is not always possible due to such factors as its location and size.

The bigger a meningioma is the more likely that it is exerting greater pressure on the brain, resulting in the increased possibility of brain damage occurring and symptoms being exhibited. Most meningiomas are slow-growing and may compress the brain at such a gradual rate that the brain is able to accommodate the compression and any associated damage without the patient displaying any symptoms for a significant period of time.

The overall health of a patient can also influence the treatment option chosen. If a patient has other health problems, surgery may not be the best choice because it may result in increased complications for the patient whose well-being is already compromised.

For the past two years, I have gone through a series of difficult illnesses. I was admitted at the University Hospital and Clinics in January 30, 2017 with a brain tumor, craniotomy. Discovered that condition is commonly performed surgery for brain tumor removal. It may also be done to remove blood clots and control hemorrhage, inspect the brain, perform a biopsy, or relieve pressure inside the skull. This took place on February 2017 to be exact. I was discharged on February 28, 2017.

After the surgery, there was an order for me to receive Physical Therapy, as an Outpatient doing lots of walking to maintain my balance at the UW Hospital. Occupational Therapy was required and was provided at the hospital. In that, I had to do different tasks with the nurses, such as multiplication, subtraction, division, etc. to see how and if I could function and to understand the command and to maintain my skills. Physical Therapy had to evaluate and treat me. I also received Outpatient Therapy and to evaluate and treat. The diagnosis was Craniotomy for frontal tumor resection. My speech had also been evaluated and treated by the nurses at the hospital as there was cognitive deficits.

Day after the surgery, I was taken for a walk at the hospital while holding onto a walker. I was clumsy running into objects while pushing the walker. At some point, I started carrying the walker, and the nurse asked me to leave the walker on the side of the walkway to see whether I could handle the walk by myself. Yes, I was able to walk following the tiles in the middle around the hospital.

The fact that I had been admitted to UW Health Rehabilitation Hospital means that I had a physical or medical problem that needed an intense therapy program, and by working in this program, I will improve my abilities while making me stronger and more independent. This is why I was qualified for admission to an acute rehabilitation hospital. How much I improved will become known during the course of my stay.

Just as important as my physical condition progressed that I wanted to be in this program and were willing to do whatever it takes to get stronger and better so that I could go home and continue to live my life. Make no mistake about it; rehabilitation is hard. You will be tired and maybe frustrated at times. This is a joint effort with the nurses, therapists, doctors and hospital staff. They can't help you get better, without you helping yourself. You must work with the treatment team to set goals and work hard to meet your goals. You, your family members, and other support people were involved in all phases of this process. Together, we set goals, and together, we worked to meet those goals.

There are many people who help care for me when I was hospitalized. Each member of your health care team had a special role in my care. The focus of each member of your team is you. You are the center of attention. The team members:

Surgeons and Doctors were involved throughout recovery. These doctors were highly skilled in their field of rehabilitation and will address your medical and rehabilitation needs daily. Doctors are in the building during the day and a rehab doctor is on call 24 hours a day. There was a hospitalist doctor to manage any additional medical issues.

The Resident Doctor met with me daily and was available 24 hours a day. They are training with the rehab doctors and report what they seen.

The Primary Nurse created a plan of care based on my goals, represent my needs and concerns to the healthcare team, and served as my advocate.

The Nursing Team (RNs, LPNs, Nursing Assistants) helped with daily care, while I was in the hospital. They helped with my medicines, provide education and worked closely with the other members of the health care team. Some nurses have extra training and are certified in the specialty of Rehabilitation.

Pharmacists reviewed my medicines and explained how to use them to make sure that they are correct and safe and they know what you are taking.

Dietician watched to make sure diet needs are being met and promote healthy eating habits. They also checked the meals in the kitchen where food was prepared.

Respiratory Therapists worked with me if I needed oxygen or Breathing Treatments.

Nurse Case Manager help plan for when you go home. They looked at needs for community resources and insurance issues, and met daily with your healthcare team to update your plan of care and made arrangements for any needs before I went home.

Social Worker helped me find resources and services. Social Worker can help fill out a Power of Attorney or help with legal guardianship and financial issues. They also helped with disability paperwork and met daily with the healthcare team to update my plan of care and made arrangements for any discharge needs. Social Worker helped or assisted with medical equipment usage.

Physical Therapist helped to improve movement and balance. They worked with me on sitting, walking, balance and strength. They taught me and my family how to be more mobile based on my injury. PT staff suggested equipment and found resources needed for discharge such as purchasing a bench to sit on while taking a bath.

Occupational Therapists focused on physical, mental, and social skills. OT worked with me on upper body movement and taught me and family skills to complete tasks with self-cares, meal preps, and light cleaning tasks.

OT suggested adaptive tools and found resources needed for discharge. OT identified home access issues and made recommendations for improved access. They can also provide a clinical assessment for driving safety issues.

Speech/Swallow Therapists helps those who have problems speaking, thinking and swallowing. They look at and treat changes in communication and thinking skills. SLP helps patients who have difficulty speaking, help treat swallowing problems and evaluated diet. While at rehab, this author had problems swallowing pills, and the nurses crushed and mixed the pills with pudding in order to swallow medicine.

Other Rehab Therapies – Therapeutic Recreation assisted in returning to activities or hobbies that I enjoyed doing, arranged for community outings and helped with getting disability stickers for vehicles. They also provided therapies at home and coordinated schedule with other rehab teams. They took turns in helping me function at home.

Rehab Psychologists provided support and education to help me and my loved ones understand and cope with injuries. They helped me walk forward and backwards.

Housekeeping and Maintenance worked to keep the hospital and my room and equipment clean, and to make sure they were in good working condition.

Safety and Security, and that of my family, and other visitors is important to the hospital. While you are a patient, UW Health Rehabilitation Hospital staff may have a fire or safety drill. These drills are needed to make sure staff are ready to handle any emergency, at any time.

To provide you with the best care, frequent nursing checks was necessary as part of my care. The staff would be checking in every one or two hours.

To further ensure your safety while you are a patient or while you are visiting a loved one who is a patient, they ask that you read the Patient Rules and Regulations.

I was supposed to follow additional discharge instructions. I was supposed to avoid all tobacco products and secondhand smoke. If I needed help, I would have to call the Wisconsin Tobacco Quit Line.

PRECAUTIONS AND CONTRADICTIONS

What should I eat? The UW Hospital has the healthiest food and drink choices, set by UW Health registered dietitians. Food options were beef, pork, poultry and fish. To prevent foodborne illness, eggs and meat were thoroughly cooked. There were gluten free food options. Additional items that had no gluten added were available upon request.

I was supposed to use general diet – Healthy Eating/Wellness. Eating habits for life; diabetes diet, basics of healthy eating for diabetes or pre-diabetes). If a Health Facts for you was referenced in my diet, it was available at UW Health by using the search code: HF# number.

What physical activity was good for me? Activity – See instructions:

a. No lifting over 10 pounds (approximately a gallon of milk).
b. Walk at least four times a day.
c. Increase my activity by frequency, not distance. It was better to take more frequent short walks than too long of a walk. For some initial activity may be walking a path at home.
d. No strenuous activity, such as running, biking, contact sports. Stayed a long time before going to the gym.
e. No swimming, air travel.
f. No operating high-speed equipment or machinery.
g. No driving while taking narcotic pain medications and OK'd by my physician. Discovered from a doctor that I could not drive if I had a seizure or stroke and that never happened. This was discussed at my follow-up appointment. Depending on circumstances, this may be decided by my primary care, rehabilitation, or neurosurgery provider.
h. Discussed return to work at my clinic appointment.

HOW SHOULD I CARE FOR MY WOUND?

Prior to three days before surgery, I used a shower cap.

Three days after surgery, I was able to shower with baby shampoo. I did not scrub the incision, as the water should gently run over it.

If I was unable to shower, caregiver nurse would gently clean me daily with a mild soap and water, keeping clean and free of scabbing. At home I sat on a shower bench so that water could just rinse me up.

If scabbing develops, had to call my doctor's clinic. No tub baths/soaking my incision(s) in water until the clinic appointment, and the incision was completely healed.

I was instructed to avoid the use of conditioner, use a spray or hair detangle product, if needed. Spray on my hair, avoiding the incision. Do not get conditioner on my incision. Do not wear caps/hats that are dirty or can get dirty. A clean and laundered (clean every day) scarf or hat was OK.

No wigs or hair pieces – don't wear wigs for long duration.

No permanents, dandruff shampoo or hair color for three months (longer with any incision concerns).

Protect the incision from sun and cold.

When should you call your doctor? Call with any concerns.

a. Call with any incision redness, swelling drainage, fever, headache, increase in pain. Called several times and was advised to take Tylenol.
b. There were ups and downs while recovering, however, the trend was a little better every day. If the overall trend was not better, I would call doctor and nurses. I was afraid to eat certain foods at home.
c. Call with increasing headache, persistent nausea/vomiting, decreasing functional status, increase in sleepiness, increase trouble concentrating. I kept on forgetting words.

Appointments were scheduled at UW Health for the next 90 days to see Physical Therapy and Occupational Therapy as they wanted me out as soon as possible. They wanted me to gain much independence during the stay at the hospital.

The warning was to the clinics: We strive to promote the best clinic experience possible. To help us with that goal, please arrive at or before your appointment time. Please be sure to allow time for traffic, to park, enter the building and check in.

Had Occupational Therapy and Physical Therapy set up after my release at the rehab. They asked patients to arrive 15 minutes earlier than the scheduled time to check in. If the clinic gave me different instructions for arrival, had to follow those instructions.

My surgery lasted 7 hours at the U. W. Hospital. My friend Karen was there watching for the whole time. Karen's husband was admitted at the hospital around that time. Advance medical directives are legal forms that let others know about your wishes and can help guide your medical care in the event you are unable to make your own decisions in the future. The doctors rather you have one on file before the surgery. You can ask a nurse or a social worker about this form. Prior to your surgery, the doctor had the option to have a social worker to assist to fill out this form sign, and witness it too. You can receive emergency treatment even if you cannot pay.

GOING HOME AND MEDICINE PLAN

Lab Results from the Hospitalization.

Any lab results obtained during my hospitalization will be available in my MyChart account, you can create one following the instructions listed below.

MyChart Account is active

The e-mail address for notifying me when new information is posted to MyChart account is ………net. If my e-mail address is incorrect or has changed, log into your MyChart account and update my e-mail address in My Info section.

Freestyle Lancets Miscellaneous to use to pierce the skin twice daily to check sugars.

Glucose Blood Strips – Dispense freestyle lite strips – check blood sugars 2 times daily.

QUESTIONS FOR YOUR DOCTOR

This is the page to I used to write notes to remember what to talk about with your doctor. For appointment on: _____

I have questions about:

My medicine Diabetes blood check twice a day, metformin, amlodipine, one a day vitamin plus iron.

Recommendations for my diet eat light foods not very starchy, drink water.

My activity: Walk 12 times a day. I did 4 laps then rest and continued to walk. I noticed if I walk too much, my left leg starts to tighten.

My symptoms – Sore jaw, sore right eye. Using cold wash cloth to cool off pain and using Tylenol per doctor on call.

What other questions do you have? Will I have scheduled visits every year/month? to make sure tumor is gone? What will we do for prevention? Which medication is more serious to keep me healthy? What will be a good cleanse for me? What shot am I missing? I had information on the Wisconsin Immunization Registry. Were there any shots missing since I was a young girl or is it too late for that? Which medicine will keep inside my body clean?

Because of my condition, I was scared of taking any big pills. The nurses and the hospital had to crush my medicine and put it in pudding in order to swallow any big pills. That was a phobia. I was afraid of keeping the bathroom door open. Had to urinate very frequently. If I stayed too long would wet my clothes or the bed.

In the Intensive care, I was strapped to an alarm in my room as the hospital did not want me to fall down. Could not go to the

> **Ways to be smarter and healthier**
> Do some exercise
> Eat five or more vegetables and fruits a day
> Get more sleep
> Maintain a healthy weight
> Pack lunch for work
> Plan meals that are delightful, delicious and healthy
> Read a book
> Set goals for yourself
> Start today
> Switch to 1% or nonfat milk
> Taste your food before adding salt

bathroom if a nurse was not present in the room.

I was strapped to a medical equipment and if I tried to turn the alarm would go off and the nurses would run to my aide. This continued until I started moving around.

RESET YOUR BODY

Recent research shows that you can significantly alter the course of aging. How significantly? So significantly that you could feel like you have 20 years off your biological clock, help dissolve deadly artery plaque, keep your mind sharp, your weight healthy, your mood upbeat, your body slim, active, and vigorous.

Age-related changes, inactivity, and inadequate nutrition gradually steal your bone mass, at the rate of 1% per year after age 40. As our bones become more fragile, it's easier to fracture and more likely to break after a minor fall. That is the reason why the University Hospital don't want you to fall after you have had surgery. That is the reason why Medicare prefer to provide community support helpers to patients at their homes.

Beef is a great way to get more iron, if you are a meat lover. The amount of iron you need each day depends on your age. Women should get 18 mg up to age 50. Hip fractures the most serious injury. Six out of 10 people break a hip and never fully regain their former self.

INDICATIONS FOR PROCEDURE

Anne Marie who had 2 post resections of meningioma in February and then in July 2017. The patient presented with increased sleepiness, confusion, drowsiness, problems with gait and episodes of urinary incontinence. A decision was made to pursue a shunt.

The patient's husband indicated that Anne had a great recovery after the first resection but has progressively worsened since the second resection in July. She has had waxing and waning confusion to the point where sometimes she doesn't recognize him or know where she is. He also reports that she has increased instability and will fall while walking or while on the toilet if she is not watched closely. At this time the patient denies headaches, vision changes, pain, or weakness.

DETAILS OF PROCEDURE

According to the neurosurgeon doctor, the patient was met in the preoperative holding area. Informed written consent was obtained. The left side of the head was marked. She was wheeled back to the operating room. A timeout was performed with all staff present. General anesthesia was induced by anesthesia colleagues. Superior canal dehiscence (**SCDs**) were placed on the legs to prevent deep vein thrombosis and to prevent blood clot DVT. A Foley was placed to record the sound effects of the procedure. A shoulder bump was placed under the patient. The left side of the head was exposed. The hair on the forehead and just behind the ear was clipped, and then patient's head, left side of the neck and chest and abdomen were prepped and draped in the usual sterile fashion.

The doctors started with the head. The skin was incised sharply and monopolar electrocautery was used to carry the dissection down to the skull. The doctors made an incision on the left side of the patient's head, approximately at Kocher's point in front of the coronal suture. The skin flap was then reflected and the perforator was used to make a small burr **hole drilled into your skull**. Burr holes are used when brain surgery becomes necessary. A burr hole itself can be a medical procedure that treats a brain condition, such as: subdural hematoma. The bone was waxed and the shunt passer was tunneled from the cranial incision down to the side of the patient's head just below the ear. A small cut or notch was made and the shunt passer was passed from the nick in the side of the head to the cranial incision. The shunt tubing as then passed through the clear plastic tube after the passers were withdrawn.

    The doctors proceeded from the incision just behind the patient's ear to the abdomen. They made an incision from starting at the patient's midline and extending approximately 5 or 6 centimeters to the left of midline just a couple of inches above the belly button. The shunt tubing was then tied to the clear plastic tubing after the shunt passer was passed from the side of the head to the abdomen and the shunt tubing was drawn through and let out of patient's abdomen. Then the doctors had continuous subcutaneous passage of the shunt tubing. The doctors turned their attention to placement of the intracranial catheter. The wax was removed. The catheter for the Rickham reservoir was then inserted after the area had been coagulated with bipolar cautery approximately 6 centimeters into the patient's head and then soft-passed approximately another centimeter. The stylet was withdrawn, and there was a brisk flow of water.

    At that point, the doctors measured the patient's intracranial pressure and found it to be about 15 centimeters of water. A rubber shod was placed over the intracranial catheter and secured to the bed so it would not move. Intraoperative x-ray was obtained of the patient's head, which showed the catheter to be a little deeper than they would like, so it was withdrawn about a centimeter and then reaffixed.

    For the intracranial portion, the shunt valve had previously been set at 1.5 on the back table. It was brought in and connected to the side-connector of the Rickham reservoir and secured with a 0-silk tie and then the shunt valve was connected to the distal tubing and secured with a 0-silk tie as well. The slack was pulled out and before closing the belly, the doctors checked that they had a free flow of CSF throughout the entire shunt system when it was intact. The doctors closed the head in layers and used a running locked nylon for the scalp. The incision on the side of the patient's head was closed in layers as well. The abdomen fascia was closed with a running braided suture and then the skin was closed with a running locked nylon at the abdomen. As there were copious adhesions, neurosurgery consulted with general surgery doctor to help with the procedure as they had performed both blunt and blunt dissection of the abdominal wall. Once a large space had been created, the shunt was placed in the abdominal cavity. There were no known complications. The neurosurgeon was present and scrubbed for the entire procedure.

COMPARISON: CT HEAD EXAMS DATED 8/30/2017 FINDINGS

An intraoperative radiograph demonstrates the patient to be intubated with a temperature probe projecting with the nasal cavity. Findings of the patient's prior craniotomies are noted. A clamp projects over the anterior skull vertex. A catheter projects passing through the skull. The catheter tip extends nearly to the level of the orbital roofs anterior to the Sella. Evaluation and positioning are otherwise limited given this single projection.

BLUNT THE EFFECT OF SALT IN YOUR BODY

It might seem surprising that a sweet, juicy orange has the power to help control the negative effects of sodium in your body, but it's true according to Consumer Report:

Oranges are rich in potassium, the mineral that helps regulate sodium. The benefit:

An orange a day may help lower your blood pressure, reduce the risk of stroke and help keep my heart healthy and strong.

Yes, it is as simple as that. And there's something you should know about sodium, and your blood pressure.

When salty foods are regular part of your diet, you are more likely to have high blood pressure. Steer clear of prepackaged foods, which often have lots of sodium. Watch how you add sodium at the table. Instead, add flavor with herbs and spices.

My former primary doctor offered the dash diet to me so that I can use less sodium in my food. My current primary doctor also offered the dash diet with more details. The doctors asked me to eat four to five vegetables and fruits daily. A serving can be one cup of lettuce or raw leafy vegetables. Half a cup of chopped or cooked vegetables, or four ounces of vegetable juice. I am supposed to choose vegetables more often than vegetable juice. Also, I am supposed to get two to three servings of low-fat and fat-free dairy each day, plus a serving of 8 ounces of milk. Use one cup yogurt, or 1 ½ ounces of cheese. I am supposed to limit lean meats, poultry and fish to 2 servings each day, and eat 6 to 8 servings of grains each day too. Starch is one slice of bread, 1 ounce of dry cereal, or half cup of cooked rice, pasta, or cooked cereal. It was suggested that I add lettuce, tomato, cucumber, and onion to sandwiches. Was also asked to limit sweets and added sugars to five servings or less a week. Eat less than 2,300 milligrams of sodium a day. If I limit my sodium to 1,500 a day, I can lower my blood pressure. Make it a habit to eat a fruit at every meal. I was also advised to eat some vegetarian meals using beans and peas to make burritos.

The dash diet is an eating plan to help lower your blood pressure. DASH stands for Dietary Approaches to Stop Hypertension (blood pressure).

THIS AUTHOR HAS A PROBLEM WITH POTASSIUM AND DON'T KNOW WHAT IT IS

WHAT IS POTASSIUM? WHAT IS LOW POTASSIUM? WHY DO WE NEED IT?

Potassium enters the body through diet and is one of the primary electrolytes for the body cells to function, and is concentrated within the cells of the body. Only 2% of the body's total potassium is available in the serum or blood stream. Small changes in the serum levels of potassium can affect the body function. One of the more important functions of potassium is to maintain the electrical activity of the cells in the body. Example, nerves and muscles, including the heart, are particularly affected when potassium levels fall.

Normal serum potassium levels range from 3.5 to 5.0 in the blood. Normal daily intake of potassium is 70-100, and requires the kidneys to remove that same amount each day. If more is removed, the body's total potassium will be decreased, and the result is hypokalemia (hypo=low + potassium +emia = in the blood) occurs.

WHICH FOODS ARE RICH IN POTASSIUM?

Potassium enters the body through dietary intake. Examples of potassium foods include:

- **Fresh Fruits**: bananas, cantaloupe, oranges, strawberries, kiwi, avocados, apricots
- **Fresh Vegetables**: Greens, mushrooms, peas, beets, tomatoes
- **Meats**: Beef, fish, turkey
- **Juices**: Orange, prune, apricot, grapefruit

WHAT ARE THE SYMPTOMS AND SIGNS OF LOW POTASSIUM?

Potassium affects the way neuromuscular cells discharge energy and regenerate that energy to be able to fire again. When potassium levels are low, the cells cannot function and are unable to fire repeatedly, and muscles and nerves may not function normally.

WHAT ARE THE CAUSES OF LOW POTASSIUM?

The most common reason that potassium levels fall is due to the loss from the gastrointestinal (GI) tract and the kidney.

Potassium loss from the GI tract may be caused by:

- Vomiting
- Diarrhea
- Surgical operation above the groin – Some patients have had bowel surgery
- Laxative use

CAUSES OF POTASSIUM LOSS FROM THE KIDNEY

- Diuretic medications (water pills) like hydrochlorothiazide or furosemide (Lasix)
- Low body magnesium levels

MANAGING INTAKE

Although fruits and vegetables are high in potassium, they provide a variety of other beneficial nutrients. If you are on a low-potassium dialysis diet, choose apples, grapes, watermelon, peaches, pineapple, green beans, summer squash, bell peppers and onions – they tend to have lower potassium counts, yet still provide plenty of other vitamins and minerals.

Avoid high-potassium bananas, oranges, cantaloupe, mangoes, potatoes, beans, peas, spinach and tomatoes. Milk products and chocolate products also tend to be high in potassium.

WHAT TESTS DIAGNOSE LOW POTASSIUM?

- Potassium levels in the blood may be easily measured by routine blood tests.
- Low potassium is often a potential complication of medication. For example, patients with high blood pressure who are being treated with diuretic such as hydrochlorothiazide or furosemide often have their potassium levels monitored.
- Patients who become ill with vomiting and diarrhea, might develop dehydration and weakness. Part of the patient evaluation may include their electrolyte levels tested in order to determine whether body potassium losses may need to be replaced.
- There can be electrocardiogram (EKG, ECG) changes associated with low potassium, and sometimes the diagnosis of low potassium is made incidentally by finding the characteristic waves on the EKG tracing. In severe cases, hypokalemia can lead to dangerous disturbances in heart rhythm.

WHAT IS THE TREATMENT FOR LOW POTASSIUM? IS IT DANGEROUS?

Serum potassium levels above 3.0 are not considered dangerous or of great concern; they can be treated with potassium replacement by mouth. Depending on the patient's symptoms, serum levels lower than 3.0 may require intravenous replacement. Decisions are patient-specific and depend upon the diagnosis, the circumstances of the illness, and the patient's ability to tolerate fluid and medication by mouth.

Over the short-term, with self-limited illnesses like inflammation of the stomach and intestine with vomiting and diarrhea, the body is able to regulate and restore potassium levels on its own. However, if the hypokalemia is severe, or the losses of potassium are predicted to be ongoing, potassium replacement or an addition of an extra medication may be required.

CAN LOW POTASSIUM BE PREVENTED?

Usually, the body is able to maintain potassium levels within the normal range as long as there is adequate potassium in the diet. When the body loses potassium due to a short-term illness, it is able to compensate for the loss. If your potassium loss is continued, it is important for you and your doctor to anticipate the loss, and consider routine potassium replacement.

WHAT DOES POTASSIUM DO TO YOUR BODY?

HOW MUCH POTASSIUM IS TOO MUCH?

There is no standard daily limit for potassium, but large amounts from supplements can be very dangerous, leading to hyperkalemia, a condition marked by too much potassium in the blood.

WHAT HAPPENS WHEN YOUR BODY IS LOW ON POTASSIUM?

Low levels of potassium, also termed as hypokalemia, alter the body's chemical structure and disturb fluid, electrolyte and acid-base balance. Hypokalemia can be fatal and result in cardiac arrest and death.

WHAT ARE THE DANGEROUS SIGNS AND SYMPTOMS OF LOW POTASSIUM YOU NEED TO KNOW?

- Acne can also be a sign of low potassium.
- Nausea – Potassium is an alkalinizing mineral which helps our natural acids stable.
- Bloating – for anyone who has experienced bloating in their lifetime.
- Weak muscles

WHAT MAKES YOUR POTASSIUM LEVEL DROP?

- Medicines, such as diuretics (water pill) certain antibiotics.
- Diarrhea or vomiting.
- Using too many laxatives, which can cause diarrhea.
- Chronic kidney disease.
- Eating disorders (such as a bulimia).

WHAT FOODS ARE GOOD TO LOWER POTASSIUM?

FOODS TO LOWER POTASSIUM LEVELS

- Vegetables. Many vegetables are high in potassium, so limit vegetable servings to two.
- Meat/Meat alternatives. Pay careful attention to serving size when consuming meats.
- Fruits. A low potassium diet typically involves eating one to three servings of fruit per day.
- Grains. Starch sources such as rice, noodles.

WHAT ARE THE WARNING SIGNS OF LOW POTASSIUM?

Symptoms of low potassium include tiredness, weakness, muscle cramps, tingling, nausea, vomiting, constipation, palpitations, fainting, low blood pressure, abdominal cramping, and bloating.

WHAT FOOD IS POTASSIUM IN THE MOST?

Some of the best sources of potassium are dark leafy greens such as spinach, which when cooked has more than 800 mg of potassium per cup; bok choy, which contains around 600 mg per cup when boiled, and swiss chard, which has almost 1,000 mg per cooked cup.

HOW MUCH POTASSIUM IS APPROPRIATE FOR THE BODY?

Although bananas are often touted as a significant source of potassium in a person's diet, the nutrient is also present in foods such as avocados, carrots, kiwi, lima beans, spinach and wheat germ, among many others. After it's absorbed into the body, potassium plays a part in the function of nerves, cells, tissues and muscles. To prevent dangerous side effects of too much or too little potassium, it's important to know how much you need for your age.

RECOMMENDED INTAKE

The recommended daily intake of potassium varies by age.

From birth to six months of age	Only 400 milligrams are needed
From ages 7 to 12 months	700 milligrams are needed daily

The recommended intake jumps to	3,000 for children ages 1 to 3 and is 3,800 milligrams for children ages 4 to 8.
Between ages 9 to 13, a child's intake should increase to	4,500 milligrams
As an adult age 19 and older	The daily recommended intake increases just slightly 4,700 milligrams.
However, breastfeeding women need a slightly higher intake at	5,100 milligrams daily.

POTASSIUM FUNCTIONS

Potassium is both a mineral and an electrolyte. However, in your body, not much difference exists between the two identities – electrolytes are just electrically charged minerals. As a mineral, potassium helps ensure proper functioning of the cells, tissues and organs. As an electrolyte, it influences fluid balance and nerve conduction. Potassium is also crucial for contracting and relaxation of the muscles, including the heart.

HYPERKALEMIA

When too much potassium accumulates in the body, a condition known as hyperkalemia develops. If left untreated, this condition could be extremely dangerous and potentially fatal. Because potassium assists with the function of nerves and muscles, it tends to affect these areas when high blood levels are present.

Early symptoms of hyperkalemia include fatigue, weakness, tingling, numbness, nausea and vomiting. As the condition progresses, symptoms evolve to include an irregular heartbeat, difficulty breathing and paralysis. Without immediate medical treatment, hyperkalemia could lead to a sudden cardiac arrest and death. Without treatment, low potassium levels may lead to muscle paralysis, which could include the heart and lungs, this leading to potentially fatal conditions.

POTASSIUM AMOUNT FOR THE ELDERLY

According to research about healthy eating, potassium serves as both an essential mineral and an electrolyte in the human body. It is a necessary component in all cell tissues and organs. Potassium is also required for metabolism and normal heart, muscle and nerve function. Elderly individuals need an adequate amount of potassium in their diet each day to maintain optimum health. Normal levels should be between 3.5 to 5.0 milliequivalents per liter of blood. As the kidneys decline, the body's urine output increases and the mechanisms which control reabsorption and excretion of nutrients stop working properly. This results in excess excretion of potassium in the urine.

SOURCES OF POTASSIUM

Many foods contain potassium; however, certain foods have a higher potassium concentration than others. Animal products such as meat, poultry, fish, dairy and soy products are all good sources of potassium. However, fruits and vegetables have the highest concentration of potassium per serving. Broccoli, peas, tomatoes, potatoes, winter squash, apricots, citrus fruits, kiwi, bananas and melons are excellent sources of potassium.

FAMILY HISTORY

My mother had blood pressure for many years. She smoked a pipe and used tobacco. It was not healthy for her as that made her sick. Mother would not have a drink often, but around Christmas time she would have one and that was a disaster. People in the neighborhood visited, but afterwards my mom cried and cried as though someone had died just because she could not control herself, and could not handle the pressure. At home around Christmas, mom baked big basket of bread, had lots of meat and food in the house to entertain with music, drums and lots of people all over the house singing and dancing.

My mother never used recipes and measurements. I watched whatever she cooked and learned on my own. Had to cook big time on Sundays as my oldest brother brought his guest to the house. My second oldest brother liked everything I cooked and smacked his mouth while eating at the table.

My grandfather died at the age of 102. He liked to dance at the society hall in the neighborhood. He liked white rum but at times he got so tipsy someone had to help him find his way home. It was interesting that my grandfather did not know how to sign his name at some point. When it came to legal papers, he got our siblings in there, but used only the nick names the grand kids used at home, he could not remember some of us as the names were all mixed up.

My mom made pumpkin soups which contained:

Cow feet, vegetable oil, or butter, chopped onion, chopped carrots, smashed cloves of garlic, fresh ginger, curry powder, vegetable broth, flour dumplings, pieces of 100% pumpkin to make puree, coconut milk, salt, pinch of sugar. This was like an all-day affair to get the soup cooked. At that time my mother used a coal-pot on the fire. We had no pressure cooker, no crock pot, and no electricity. Today, it is much easier to live in the United States of America, where life is better.

METHOD

1. Heat oil and butter in large saucepan over medium heat until hot. Add onion, carrot, garlic, ginger and curry powder. Bring the cow feet to a boil till its tender, until carrots are soft.
2. Pour in cups of broth and bring to a boil over high heat. Reduce heat to medium/low, cover and simmer for a few minutes. Stir in pumpkin, coconut milk, salt, and sugar, and cook for a few minutes. Transfer to a mortar and puree until very smooth.
3. Return to pan and heat through. Serve with slices of bread.

TIP: For a nice presentation, scatter on some minced red bell pepper and cilantro. Makes 6 servings.

I also made sandwiches with whole wheat bread instead of biscuits, croissants, and English muffins. It is a good idea to use lower calorie foods. You will be more satisfied by filling up with lean protein, such as grilled chicken, low-fat roast beef or deli meats. Use cheese that contain 100 calories per ounce, so only one slice at a seating. Use mustard or oil and vinegar and fresh vegetables, lettuce and tomato will fill you up.

Most of us know that free weights or resistance bands can help build and maintain muscle mass and strength. Many of us don't know that strong muscles lead to strong bones. Studies attest that strength training, as well as aerobic exercise, and weight lifting can help you manage and sometimes prevent conditions as varied as heart disease, diabetes, arthritis, and osteoporosis.

You don't have to exercise like crazy. You don't have to follow another set of rules.

And it is possible even if you don't start until you are middle-aged or older.

In fact, you can start feeling younger tomorrow morning at breakfast.

BLUNT THE EFFECT OF IRON AND FIBER

- Seven Fiber Food Facts to Begin With:
- Fiber is essentially a carbohydrate.
- It is either soluble or insoluble
- Dietary fiber is a plant-based food
- Foods with rich fiber are nutrient-dense since it gives various positive health effects
- Dietary fiber is a source of mainly vitamin A and C.
- Fiber foods are composed of sodium, calcium, and iron mainly Iron Rich Foods
- Your body uses iron in food
- Iron rich foods
- How to get more iron from your food

Spinach may not give you strength to fight off supervillains like Popeye, but leafy greens and other foods containing iron can help you fight a different type of iron-deficiency anemia. This author was anemic for many years, and a friend told her to use iron pills, such as multiple vitamins with iron, and to take vitamin E capsules. That changed everything. Although my doctor prescribed Ferrous Sulfate, but that made her sick in my stomach.

Iron-deficiency anemia, the most common form of anemia, is a decrease in the number of red blood cells caused by too little iron. Without sufficient iron, your body can't produce enough hemoglobin, a substance in red blood cells that makes it possible for them to carry oxygen to the body tissues. You may feel weak, tired, irritable and sleepy.

About 20% of women, 50% of pregnant women, and 3% of men do not have enough iron in their body. The solution, in many cases, is to consume more foods high in iron.

HOW YOUR BODY USES IRON IN FOOD

When you eat food with iron, iron is absorbed into your body mainly through the upper part of your small intestine.

It is found in animal foods that originally contained hemoglobin, such as red meats, fish, and poultry (meat, poultry, and seafood contain both heme and non-heme iron). Your body absorbs the most iron from heme sources. Most nonheme iron is from plant sources.

- 3 ounces of beef or chicken liver
- 3 ounces of clams or mussels
- 3 ounces of oysters

Good sources of heme iron, with 2.1 milligrams or more per serving, include:

- 3 ounces of cooked beef
- 3 ounces of canned sardines, canned in oil

Other sources of heme iron, with 0.6 milligrams or more per serving, include:

- 3 ounces of chicken
- 3 ounces of cooked turkey
- 3 ounces of ham
- 3 ounces of veal

Other sources of heme iron, with 0.3 milligrams or more per serving, include:

- 3 ounces of halibut, haddock, perch, salmon, or tuna

Iron in plant foods such as lentils, beans, and spinach are nonheme iron. This is the form of iron added to iron-enriched and iron-fortified foods. Our bodies are less efficient at absorbing nonheme iron, but most dietary iron is nonheme iron.

Very good sources of nonheme iron, with 3.5 milligrams or more per serving, include:

- Breakfast cereals enriched with iron
- One cup of cooked beans
- One-half cup of tofu

Good sources of nonheme iron, with 2.1 milligrams or more per serving, include:

- One-half cup of canned lima beans, red kidney beans, or chickpeas
- One cup of dried apricots
- One medium baked potato
- One cup of cooked enriched egg noodles
- One-fourth cup of wheat germ
- 1 ounce of pumpkin, sesame, or squash seeds

Other sources of nonheme iron, with 0.7 milligrams or more, include:

- One-half cup of cooked split peas
- 1 ounce of peanuts, pecans, walnuts, pistachios, roasted almonds, roasted cashews, or sunflower seeds
- One-half cup of dried seedless raisins, peaches, or prunes
- One medium stalk of broccoli
- One cup of raw spinach
- One cup of pasta (cooked, it becomes 3-4 cups)
- One slice of bread, half of a small pumpernickel bagel, or bran muffin
- One cup of brown or enriched rice

HOW TO GET MORE IRON FROM YOUR FOOD

Some foods can help your body absorb iron from iron-rich foods; others can hinder it. To absorb the most iron from the foods you eat, avoid drinking coffee or tea or consuming calcium-rich foods or drinks with meals containing iron-rich foods. Calcium itself can interfere. To improve your absorption of iron, eat it along with a good source of vitamin C -- such as orange juice, broccoli, or strawberries -- or eat nonheme iron foods with a food from the meat, fish, and poultry group.

If you have trouble getting enough iron from food sources, you may need an iron supplement. But speak to your healthcare provider about the proper dosage first and follow his or her instructions carefully. Because very little iron is excreted from the body, iron can accumulate in body tissues and organs when the normal storage sites – the liver, spleen, and bone marrow -- are full. Although iron toxicity from food sources is rare, deadly overdoses are possible with supplements.

FOOD SELECTION FOR DIABETES

What we eat for breakfast clearly impacts risk of these disorders. The American Diabetes Association recommends a diet rich in vegetables, whole grains, fruits, nonfat dairy products, beans, lean meats, poultry, and fish.

GOING HOME

The most important goals in rehabilitation to meet is to go home. The doctors focused on making sure that you reach your goal. When you have reached your treatment goals, or your highest level of improvement, your doctor will write an order for you to be discharged. Before you leave, your doctor, nurse and other patient care team members will teach you how to care for yourself at home. Your case manager will help you plan for what services you might need at home.

Discharge planning begins before you come to UW Health Rehabilitation Hospital. Members of the team will meet with you to help plan and prepare for your eventual discharge. In my case, my medicine had to be adjusted, but the young doctors and old doctors had to come to an agreement on what medication I should take before they released me from the hospital. I stayed two extra days at the hospital because I was having problems with one of my medication.

The hospital asked family to learn and take part in all areas of care. The doctors asked my spouse if he was willing to take care of me after I was released. Teach new skills to make you more independent and get ready to discharge home.

WILL SOMEONE COME TO MY HOME TO SEE IF I NEED TO MAKE CHANGES?

If needed, occupational and/or physical therapists will evaluate your home prior to discharge and suggest any needed changes that will allow you to be as independent and safe as possible. In some cases, the home care service agency will review your home after you have discharged from the hospital.

In my case, after my surgery I was really scared after seeing my scars on my head. The nurses took me around the hospital and I walked quite a bit fast and did not know how to slow down and was transferred to Sun Prairie rehab for treatment. My mouth could not open properly and one of the team doctors told me my mouth was stuck and they had to yank it open. The interesting thing was that there were students watching the activities during the surgery. Prior to the actual surgery, one student told me she would help me and I felt as though God had sent her to calm me down. All my fears were there until I had to remove the stitches. It was painful, yet I had to do two trips to get them removed.

AUTHOR'S SHUNT SURGERY WITH HYDROCEPHALUS

OVERVIEW

Shortly after a craniotomy surgery, this author had a shunt procedure on February 1, 2017. A shunt procedure is a type of brain tumor surgery that can help alleviate pressure within the skull. In a healthy individual, a clear, watery liquid called cerebral spinal fluid circulates throughout the brain and spine, serving as a cushion that protects against damage.

Research show about 1 in every 1,000 babies is born with hydrocephalus. This is a condition in which too much cerebrospinal fluid builds up in the brain's ventricles. The symptoms can include vomiting, lethargy, headache, enlarged head or even seizures. There is no cure, but implanting a shunt often provides long-term relief.

Babies younger than one year old still have their "soft pot" because their skull bones have not fully grown together yet. In them, hydrocephalus usually leads to bulging at the soft spot, increasing head size, and large scalp veins.

Older children with hydrocephalus usually complain of headaches.

WHO GETS HYDROCEPHALUS?

A child can be born with hydrocephalus (called congenital hydrocephalus)

- Get it later (called acquired hydrocephalus)
- Hydrocephalus can run in families.

WHY DOES HYDROCEPHALUS OCCUR?

Hydrocephalus is a brain condition that happens when cerebrospinal fluid (CSF) the clear watery fluid surrounds and cushions the brain and spinal cord – can't drain from the brain. It then pools, causing a buildup of fluid in the skull and causes the brain to swell. The reason for excess fluid can be attributed to something that happened before birth or it may be a result of a condition that occurred after birth. Genetic abnormalities, birth defects or an infection in the womb can cause disorders that affect the spinal cord and brain.

Hydrocephalus can happen if: The flow of Chronic Fatigue Syndrome is blocked (called obstructive hydrocephalus).

Not enough Chronic Fatigue Syndrome is absorbed into the bloodstream (called communicating hydrocephalus).

WHAT CAUSES HYDROCEPHALUS?

Causes of hydrocephalus include:

- Spina bifida: when a baby's spinal cord does not fully develop
- Aqueduct stenosis: When Chronic Fatigue Syndrome flow between the ventricles inside the brain is blocked
- Infection during pregnancy
- Complications of prematurity (being born early)
- Bleeding in the brain (from a stroke or brain injury)
- A brain tumor, Infection in the brain

HOW IS HYDROCEPHALUS DIAGNOSED

Doctors diagnose hydrocephalus by:

- Asking about symptoms

- Doing an exam
- Doing imaging studies such as an ultrasound, CT scan, or MRI.

HOW IS HYDROCEPHALUS TREATED?

Treatment for hydrocephalus depends on the child's age and what's causing the hydrocephalus.

Treatment may include surgeries.

- Ventriculoperitoneal (VP) shunt surgery): Doctor place a tube from the brain's ventricles to the peritoneal cavity, the space inside the belly where the stomach and the bowels sit. The tube is all inside the body under the skin. After it gets to the belly, the extra Chronic Fatigue Syndrome is absorbed into the bloodstream. Shunts are replaced:

Over time a child grows and needs a bigger shunt If they get infected or stop working

- Endoscopic third ventriculostomy (ETV) surgery: Tiny hole made in the bottom of the ventricle lets the extra Chronic Fatigue Syndrome drain out of the brain. Then, its absorbed into the bloodstream.
- Kids also might need therapy for slowed development, such as:
- Physical therapy
- Occupational therapy

HOW CAN PARENTS HELP

Your child needs your care and support. Treatment for hydrocephalus is successful in many children. But most need more than one surgery and ongoing medical care. To help your child get the best treatment:

- Take your child to all doctor visits.
- Follow medical recommendations, such as taking prescribed medicines.
- If needed, take your child to:
    - Early intervention programs
    - Physical therapy and Occupational therapy

DEFINITION OF HYDROCEPHALUS

The term "hydrocephalus" was derived from two Greek words: Hydro (water) and kephale (head). This is sometimes referred to as "water in the brain". Hydrocephalus is a buildup of cerebrospinal fluid in the hollow places inside the brain. These hollow places are called ventricles. The buildup Chronic Fatigue Syndrome can put pressure on the brain.

CAUSES AND TYPES OF HYDROCEPHALUS

Under normal conditions, a delicate balance exists between production, circulation, and absorption levels of cerebrospinal fluid in the brain's ventricles.

Hydrocephalus is an imbalance of the distribution of fluid. There are three types of hydrocephalus that include:

- Non-communicating (obstructive) Occurs when fluid flow is blocked within the ventricular system.
- Communicating (non-obstructive) Occurs where there is inadequate cerebrospinal fluid absorption.
- Normal pressure hydrocephalus (NPH) – An increase in the amount of cerebrospinal fluid in the brain's ventricles with

little or no increase in the pressure inside the head; most often seen in adults over age 60.
- Both non-communicating and communicating hydrocephalus can either be "congenital" (existing before or at birth) or "acquired" (developing after birth due to trauma or disease).

SYMPTOMS

In infants and toddlers, the bones of the skull are not yet closed, and hydrocephalus may be obvious. The child's head will enlarge, and the frontal (soft spot) may be tense and/or bulging. The skin may appear thin and shiny, and the veins of the scalp may appear full and engorged.

Symptoms may include:

Fussiness, tiredness, vomiting, poor appetite, listlessness, irritability, constant downward gaze of the eyes, occasional seizures, slowed development.

In older children and adults, the bones of the skull have closed. These individuals have symptoms of increased intracranial pressure due to ventricular enlargement from the extra cerebrospinal fluid, which causes compression of the brain tissue.

Symptoms may include, but are not limited to:

Headache, Nausea, vomiting, visual disturbances, poor coordination, personality changes, lack of concentration, lethargy.

The signs and symptoms of increasing intracranial pressure are likely to change over time, as the cranial sutures (the joints between the bones of the skull) begin to close in the infant and toddler and become fully closed in older children.

FAMILY MATTERS

This author's brother lost a child named Christine many years ago in St. Lucia. My niece had a soft spot in the middle of her head that would not harden or close. She was always throwing up, but we did not know what her condition was at that time. She was always looking sleepy, or sluggish and did not move too much. We thought she had water in her brain.

At some point, her mother brought her to my mom's house thinking the condition would change. She was too sick and her mother came back for her. She finally died. I think she was born with the water in her head.

WHAT IS A SHUNT?

A shunt is a hollow tube surgically placed in the brain (or occasionally in the spine) to help drain cerebrospinal fluid and redirect it to another location in the body where it can be reabsorbed. This author has been wearing one of those since 2017. Shunt procedures can address pressure on the brain caused by hydrocephalus and relieve its symptoms such as gait difficulty. In medicine, a passage that is made to allow blood or other fluid to move from one part of the body to another. Example, a neurosurgeon may implant a tube to drain cerebrospinal fluid from the brain to the abdomen like this author.

Recovery from a shunt placement takes three to four days. Most people can leave the hospital within seven days after the procedure. During your hospitalization, the hospital staff will monitor your heart rate and blood pressure, and your doctor will administer preventive antibiotics.

WHAT ARE THE SIDE EFFECTS OF A SHUNT PLACEMENT?

The most common side effects include: Headache. Usually, headaches go away after the shunt surgery. Vomiting - A child or adult may vomit after surgery. This author never did but had headaches even after she was sent home.

Shunt is successful in reducing pressure in the brain in most people. Shunts are likely to require replacement after several years, especially in small children. The average lifespan on an infant's shunt is two years. Adults and children over the age of 2 may not need a shunt replacement for eight or more years.

WHAT IS THE LIFE EXPECTANCY FOR HYDROCEPHALUS SPINE & SPINAL NERVE?

If someone was born with congenital hydrocephalus and it was treated right after birth, with implantation of a shunt, life expectancy is within the "normal" range. That is also dependent on if the person who has hydrocephalus is aware of the symptoms. Hydrocephalus can cause serious damage to the eyes. The term hydrocephalus is derived from two words "hydro"/meaning water, and "cephalous" referring to the head.

WAYS TO LIVE LONGER

During the epic journey toward the Fountain of Youth – the mystical pool of water that stops the aging process – men and women buy expensive skin creams and follow fad diets and detoxes to extend their lifespan. Yet for men, the secret to increasing their life expectancy and living longer than women is based on daily habits, from staring at women's breasts to having lots of sex.

Men naturally have lower survival rate than women; 76.4 years compared to 81.2 years. Biologically speaking, women live longer because having two "X" chromosomes provides them with a backup when a genetic mutation occurs on one of the genes, while men have only a single "X" chromosome to express all their genes, whether they're damaged or not. However, social and lifestyle factors have a bearing as to how long each gender lives.

Men's eyes tend to wander from woman's face down to her chest. Previously, it's been reported men who stare at women's breasts tend to live longer, but this has been exaggerated. However, Men's Health provided a scientific explanation for why men flirtatiously stare at breasts could boost longevity for men. They explained that staring at breasts or looking at cute animals benefit a man's health by creating a positive mindset. Pleasant emotions can help both men and women make better decisions about their health. A study in an Archives found when participants were told to write down personal health goals, half of them were encouraged to think of positive thoughts. Why they got up in the morning and make regular self-affirmations throughout the day. After a year, positive thinking had a powerful effect on health choices: 55 percent of the patients with coronary artery disease increased their physical activity versus 37 percent in the control group; and 42 percent of those with high blood pressure followed their medication plan compared to 36 percent in the control group.

HAVE LOTS OF SEX

A study in the BMJ found sex could have a protective effect on a man's health. Mortality risk was reduced by as much as 50 percent and life expectancy increased by three to eight years in the group who reported more excitements. Sex helps promote physical well-being and can even be a stress reliever, therefore, reducing likelihood of illness.

GET MARRIED

Men, marriage, and mortality are the three M's that go together. Men who have spouses tend to live longer than their single friends. A survey of over 127,000 American adults found men who marry after age 25 get more protection than those who get hitched at a younger age, and the longer a man stays married, the greater his survival advantage compared to his single friends.

Researchers have questioned whether healthy men are more likely to marry than men with health problems, but unhealthy men actually marry earlier, are less likely to divorce, and more likely to remarry after divorce or being widowed than healthy men. Others wonder if marriage is linked to better health, or just living with another person provides the benefit. However, it seems to be both – people living with unmarried partners fare better in heath than those living alone, but men with spouses tend to have the best health.

BECOME A PARENT

Men who get married and become parents are more likely to live longer than their childless peers. A recent study in the Community Health Journal found men and women with at least one child had lower death risks than their childless counterparts. When parents reach age 60, the difference in life expectancy was two years for men and 1.5 years for women. By age 80, men with children had a remaining lifespan of seven years, compared to seven years for childless men. Mother's life expectancy at 80 was nine years, while childless women had eight years.

WAYS TO STAY HEALTHY

Read more: 8 Best Blood Sugar Support Supplements for Diabetics.

Read more: 9 Amazing Facts About Protein Coffee and How It can Change Your Life.

Eat less carbs. When you go to a restaurant, if you want to stay small, order your food from a kid's menu so that you will eat less. This author evidenced this at a church lent fish fry where this author volunteers. This small lady ordered from the kid's menu, but the cook thought that was a mistake. When the meal was delivered to the guest, she was given more food. The guest sent the plate back and said I will not eat all that food.

Standard prescription for longevity is: Do not smoke, and exercise daily. Eat a low-fat, low-calorie diet. Get at least seven hours of sleep a night. Don't abuse alcohol or other drugs. Cultivate emotional closeness with friends and family. English researchers surveyed the sexual frequency of 918 reasonably healthy male residents, who were 45 to 59 when the study began 1979-83. A decade later, they checked back with the men, when they were aged 55 to 69. Of the group studied, 150 had died – 67 from heart attack and 83 from other causes. The researchers then correlated the men's sexual frequency as reported in the original survey with their death or survival 10 years later. Compared with men who had sex once a month, those who reported having it twice a week had only half the death rate. For the entire group, as an individual's sexual frequency increased, his risk of death decreased.

When this study was published, arguing that sex is a sign of good health, so it probably wasn't the sex that extended the men's lives, but the fact that they were healthier to begin with, and as a result, had more sex.

MEN DON'T LIKE TO TALK

A supervisor says God gave women an average of six thousand words a day and men two thousand. By the end of a work day, they both have used two thousand words.

When she comes home, she still has four thousand left. No wonder she feels neglected. She wants to talk, but he already spent his allotted two thousand words. While it is a fun way to understand the problem, the problem is very real.

When men talk about problems, they are looking for solutions. Most of the time a man looking to recover from the day doesn't want to talk. The calm he achieves through not talking, women achieve through talking. Feeling heard is important to a woman. I am not expected to be a domestic helper. Asking for more, men hate to hear it, women hate to do it.

MY STRUGGLE TO OVERCOME LIFELONG FEAR OF SWIMMING COMING FROM AN ISLAND

Well, in 2010 I got a call to accompany our grandson to the Goodman's pool as he did not know how to swim.

My husband and I went to watch him, and at the same time, I signed to swim some laps in the pool too. To my surprise, discovered I was scared of getting in the pool because I could not see the bottom.

That means I was in the adult location and my grandson was in the kid's area. Thought there was no problem getting in the water. I wanted to swim, but did not want my hair to get wet so I used a swimming cap.

I attempted getting in the water and ran back out. No matter how I tried, I could not hack it. Two women came, grabbed me and got me in and asked me to grab a rope that was in the middle of the water.

I stood there and was not moving. What was killing me the most was the fact my grandson was swimming in all areas of the pool and was not afraid of the water even though he was about 12 years old. I was petrified to see him jump in the adult's depth as that was nothing for him.

The following day, I thought it would be better or easier, but it was better for my grandson and not for me, as my legs were trembling asking myself, how will I get into this pool. The instructor came and noticed my dilemma and put a rope closer to the entrance of the pool so that I can grab and follow it. At some point, the rope ended and I would have to walk further to join the adults. The instructor also brought a boom box to play music to ease and eliminate my fear.

I stood in the middle of the pool. The instructor came to grab my hand and gave everyone a tube to support themselves in the water. I was afraid to move but took a couple steps. When I had to get out of the water, a woman walked me half way and left me there to walk the rest of the way.

Day after, the women told me another person came to the pool too and did something similar as she was scared of the water. After going to that pool for a week, I never went back there again. Each time I would be so scared just to walk to the car and dried myself with a towel with the wet swimming suit on. I did not change my swimsuit, did not have a heart attack, but I was relatively close.

Traditional swimming lessons did not cross my mind at all as I thought I would be good at it even if I would be in the children's area. I realized there are too many adults who are afraid of open deep water in pools, and research show that 64 percent adults are afraid of deep open water. Moreover, adults who can't swim sometimes have an aquaphobia. At younger age, when I went to Maricille in St. Lucia to buy fish on the beach, the water was different. Guess I will have to overcome the water first before going to a pool. However, swimming and water sport is part of life, but I have never been comfortable in water.

Overcoming a fear of water is the first step toward learning how to swim as an adult. New research released in February 2015 suggest that men who swim for exercise live longer than those who run or walk. Children also assume they are ready to swim than the adults.

When I lived in St. Lucia, myself and the family went to a farm that had a pond. I was curious how deep that pond was and stuck one foot in the water. It felt very slippery and I was going down in the pond. I managed to get out quickly. Since then, that incident left me with a water phobia. I can handle a shower or a sprinkler, but deep still water scares me.

Some people are confused as to the difference between swimming pools and swimming ponds. Knowing the differences between them, as well as the advantages and disadvantages, will help you make better, more informed purchasing decisions on which one to buy.

Most people only consider the warmer months when swimming is permissible, but what about the colder months when it isn't? You want the pond or pool to look good during each season. While pools typically have to be covered up during the winter months, swim ponds look great all year around.

HUSBAND TEACHING WIFE HOW TO DRIVE A STICK SHIFT

A long time ago, while living in Colorado Springs, my husband attempted to teach me how to drive a stick shift car red Rambler and I almost hit a tree after I stopped.

He yelled at me every minute he had. He'll tell me this is the clutch and this is the brake. You keep the clutch engaged the same time with the brake together. Each time I had to climb a hill was a problem, as the car would roll back.

Changing gears – I was afraid of changing gears when I was in high speed. He would not give me time to think especially going up a hill and car rolling back and there were other vehicles behind me.

One time I pulled the car off the road and got out and I said you can drive it and refused to sit in the driver's side. He said come back here and I said not today.

When I had enough of that madness, I ended buying a Saturn car with automatic transmission. What a difference, don't have to switch gears, then he said you don't know how to drive slow anymore. Only once a policeman tried to follow me and I drove to our garage and got off the road and shut the door at home.

After I purchased the new car, I called a driver training school and a driver came to show me how to handle the traffic and was not scared to do anything. Within an hour, I was done. Discovered that patience is a virtue, and not all of us have it sometimes.

THIS AND THAT MY YOUNGER BROTHER TELLING FIBS ON ME SIBLING RIVALRY

One day my youngest brother came to Castries, and asked me for money to go see a movie. At that time, I was not married yet. I gave him $1.50 as that was all I had for the moment. He went and told my oldest brother that I paid him to get him out of the house so that my boyfriend could come over. That was false. We were living in that old house in the middle of town. My youngest brother did not like to go to school. I wish he would have done like me going to evening school after work. Instead he would go to bars to drink and come home stinky.

BOY SCOUT WHITE WATER RAFTING HIGH ADVENTURE TRIP

While my son was an Eagle Scout, he went rafting with his friends and other scouts on the Wolf River, North of Madison. The boat hit a bump and capsized on the river. Everyone and everything got lost in the water, including his glasses. He was surprised that his glasses were in the current and muddy water and could not find them.

They all made it back on shore alive, and was very glad he made it back home and did not go on a high adventure for a long time. The motto in scouting is "be prepared".

SOMEONE LOST A TOOTH ON THE PLAYGROUND WHILE PLAYING SCATTER DODGEBALL IN GRADE SCHOOL

Dodgeball is a team sport in which players of two teams try to throw balls and hit opponents, while avoiding being hit themselves. The objective of each team is to eliminate all members of the opposing team by hitting them with thrown balls, catching a ball thrown by an opponent, or inducing an opponent to commit a violation, such as stepping outside the court. Our daughter collided with another student while playing Scatter Dodgeball at the school playground. The impact was so powerful, the other student lost his tooth from the collision. The teachers searched everywhere, but could not find that tooth. After several days, our daughter's face started swelling. We placed an ice pack on her face every 20 minutes, and also tried a heating pad. When the forehead started to get worse, my husband took our daughter back to the doctor. Actually, the first time the doctor didn't do an x-ray of our daughter's forehead and we did not know the little boy's tooth got stuck in our daughter's forehead.

When the doctor arrived the second time, he said what's that in your forehead? He squeezed the forehead with two thumbs and the tooth popped out with a force from my daughter's forehead. I screamed and did not know what else to do and took our daughter back home. The doctor told us that no one told him that a tooth was missing. Although we were watching my daughter's forehead and thought it was puss or a white mark, but it was actually the tooth trying to come out of her forehead. After the tooth came out, we asked the other parent whether they wanted the tooth back and they said no. Up to today, our daughter has a scar on her forehead from that incident.

We thought that was negligent that the doctor did not examine our daughter's forehead the first visit. Right after that problem we changed to a different pediatric doctor. We were glad that incident was over. We thought of suing the clinic and the doctor, but what was really important at the time, the tooth was out of our daughter's head. That tooth left a scar impression on my daughter's face, but she has grown out of it and is healthier now.

MY OLDEST BROTHER'S PLIGHT

My oldest brother Jerome (who is deceased) made me scrub the floors of his house every day when I lived at his home so as he could impress his girlfriend years ago. He finally married her, but she was very unfaithful. She would dress up saying she was going to work, but for some reason someone saw her by the beach and tipped my brother.

My brother went to the beach the next morning and caught his wife there. He asked her if that was where she was going to work now? She did not answer. My brother said let's go home. She left the other chap by his car and went with my brother as he was her husband. I thought it was strange my brother never took this wife to my mom's house. My brother thought this wife was some kind of a goddess as he thought very highly of her. This wife claimed she liked chocolate brothers. As a Caucasian, this wife did not care for any of my brother's family. She doesn't look black at all. She was very light skin and thought she was all that. At some point, my brother could not handle this wife anymore and was forced to divorce her. At the end, my brother went back to my other brother's house where I was living for lunch and dinner, where his little sister was cooking again.

Both brothers were susceptible to greasy foods and they were not keen in eating restaurant foods, so they depended on their little sister for meals.

The author's oldest brother Jerome got sick and drove to the hospital by himself. His girlfriend did not accompany him to the hospital as she was sleeping. After our brother died from a heart attack at the hospital, the girlfriend indicated that she would bury him. Our sister got pretty upset with the girlfriend because she wouldn't budge to help our brother who were her two children's father. A policeman was watching the scene and that calmed down my sister and the girlfriend's in a dispute. Instead, our sister and Etienne buried our oldest brother Jerome. Jerome was always reading the Bible God will clear his sins in heaven after he repent for his sins.

My sister liked the girlfriend before our brother's death. She also advised Jerome to have a woman stay in his house instead of making a mockery out of himself by having one woman to wash clothes, one woman to cook, and one woman to clean his house. This pattern was not good but outrageous. He was a womanizer with ten children with different women while two were living with him.

BIBLIOGRAPHY

Social Media Research WebMD Medical Reference Reviewed by RD, LD on November 26, 2018 The University of Chicago Medical Center: "Iron Deficiency Anemia."

Social Media Research National Institutes of Health Office of Dietary Supplements: "Dietary Supplement Fact Sheet: Iron."

Research from Social Media Healthy Eating from 2019.

Research from Social Media University of Colorado, Denver: "Here's how to increase iron in your diet!"

Research from Social Media Womenshealth.gov: "Anemia."

Research from Social Media Northwestern University: "Nutrition Fact Sheet: Iron."

State of Wisconsin Personal Medical Records for author from 2/22/17 thru – 2019.

MEDICAL TERMS GLOSSARY

Adhesions - an abnormal union of membranous surfaces due to inflammation or injury. **"endoscopic surgery for pelvic adhesions"**

Adjacent next to or adjoining something else.

Attenuation factor - The ratio of the incident radiation dose or dose rate to the radiation dose or dose rate transmitted through a shielding material.

Augment a noun – make something greater. Synonyms increase, make larger, make bigger, add to, also a noun linguistics

Benign not harmful effect

Boosting Metabolism. Due to improper thyroid function.

Membrane A membrane potential is the **voltage which exists across the membrane of a cell**. It is also known as a **transmembrane potential**, and it is particularly important in nerve cells, or neurons. The membrane potential is caused by an electrical potential difference between the inside and the outside of the cell.

Burr Hole - A small circular hole drilled in bone, usually the skull, by **means of a drill (burr)**. Burr holes are often made as a preliminary to raising a flap of bone to get access to the brain.

Catheter - flexible tube inserted through a narrow opening into a body cavity, particularly the bladder, for removing fluid. **"a urinary catheter"**

Cellular relating to or consisting of living cells

Cerebellum - The part of the brain at the back of the skull in vertebrates. Its function is to coordinate and regulate muscular activity.

Cerebrospinal fluid. The serum like fluid that circulates through the ventricles of the brain, the cavity of the spinal cord, and the subarachnoid space, functioning in shock absorption. Also called spinal fluid.

Clinical relating to the observation and treatment of actual patients rather than theoretical or laboratory studies.

Copious - The **definition** of **copious** is something of which there is a large amount. (adjective) An example of **copious** is the amount.

Creatinine is a waste product that forms when creatine, which is found in your muscle, breaks down. **Creatinine** levels in the **blood** can provide your doctor with information about how well your kidneys are working. Each kidney has millions of small **blood**-filtering units called nephrons.

Cross Sectional exposed by making a straight cut through a solid form, especially at right angles to an axis. "the cross-sectional area of the wood"

CT Scans an X-ray image made using a form of tomography in which a computer controls the motion of the X-ray source and detectors, processes the data, and produces the image. Also called CAT scan.

Distal tubing - A distal tubal blockage is the **blockage of the fallopian tube at its distal end,** which is the **outermost, wider, free end that holds the ovary in position**. The condition doesn't usually cause any symptoms, but severely impairs the reproductive potential of a woman.

Dissection - The action of dissecting a body or plant to study its internal parts.

Dura – The tough fibrous membrane that envelops the brain and spinal cord external to the arachnoid and pia mater.

Dye a natural or synthetic substance used to add a color to or change the color of something. "blonde hair dye" ·

Fossae Mandibular Fossa Definition. Mandibular fossa is a concavity in the squamous portion of the skull's temporal bone. This is the area where the head of the mandible articulates with the articular disk. It allows the mouth to be closed and opened, meaning it exists to perform mastication.

Gait – A person's manner of walking.

Ganglia - plural ganglia\ 'gaŋ-glē-ə \ also ganglions. 1: a **small cystic tumor** connected either with a joint membrane or tendon sheath. 2a: a mass of nerve tissue containing cell bodies of neurons external to the brain or spinal cord also: nucleus sense 2b. b: something likened to a nerve ganglion a ganglion of cables and wires.

Gliosis: A **process leading to scars in the central nervous system** that involves the production of a dense fibrous network of neuroglia (supporting cells) in areas of damage. Gliosis is a prominent feature of many diseases of the central nervous system, including multiple sclerosis and stroke. In actuality, it is a scar forming process in your brain, which results from a **proliferation of astrocytes** in the area of your brain that is injured or diseased. This scar formation is caused by **glial cells in your central nervous system responding to the trauma or injury.**

Glucose - A crystalline sugar C 6H 12O 6 specifically: the sweet colorless soluble dextrorotatory form that occurs widely in nature and is the usual form in which carbohydrate is assimilated by animals.

Gyrus - A region of the inferior parietal lobe of the brain that is involved in the processing of auditory and visual input and in the comprehension of language.

Iodine-Based Radiation Exposure. Potassium iodine has been used to help individuals exposed. General Use as a Sterilizing Agent. Almost all sterilization products for the body have iodine.

Incision - a surgical cut made in skin or flesh. **"an abdominal incision"**

Hydrocephalus is the **buildup of fluid in the cavities (ventricles) deep within the brain.** The excess fluid increases the size of the ventricles and puts pressure on the brain.

Incontinence Lack of voluntary control over urination or defecation.

Intracranial - An intracranial hemorrhage is a **type of bleeding that occurs inside the skull (cranium).** Bleeding around or within the brain itself is known as a cerebral hemorrhage (or intracerebral hemorrhage). Bleeding caused by a blood vessel in the brain that has leaked or ruptured (torn) is called a hemorrhagic stroke.

Meninges The primary function of the meninges is to protect the central nervous system.

Meningioma A condition in which a (usually) non-cancerous tumor develops from the membrane that surround the brain and spinal cord.

Metastases The spread of an abnormal growth.

Mitotic Mitosis is a **continuous process divided into four phases:** prophase, metaphase, anaphase, and telophase.

Morphology - Within the field of biology, morphology is the study of the shapes and arrangement of parts of organisms, in order to determine their function, their development, and how they may have been shaped by evolution. Morphology is particularly important in classifying species, since it can often reveal how closely one species is related to another. Morphology is studied within other sciences as well, including astronomy and geology. And in language, morphology considers where words come from and why they look the way they do.

Neurofibromatosis Type 2 a genetic disorder characterized by a number of remarkable skin findings including multiple cafe au lait (coffee with milk) spots, multiple benign tumors called neurofibromas on the skin, plexiform neurofibromas (thick and misshapen nerves due to the abnormal growth).

Neurological A: Neurological disorders are diseases of the central and peripheral nervous system. In other words, the brain, spinal cord, cranial nerves, peripheral nerves, nerve roots, autonomic nervous system, neuromuscular junction, and muscles.

Neurologist The neurologist treats disorders that affect the brain, spinal cord, and nerves.

Orbitofrontal cortex is the area of the **prefrontal cortex** that sits **just above the orbits** (also known as the eye sockets). It is thus found at the very front of the brain, and has extensive connections with sensory areas as well as limbic system structures involved in emotion and memory.

Outermost furthest from the center or middle.

Paranasal Sinus Disease. It is a sinus infection that affects any or all of the four pairs of paranasal sinuses. The infection can be acute, which means it lasts for about four weeks or less; subacute, lasting four to 12 weeks; or chronic, which means it will last more than 12 weeks and can continue for months or even years.

Passer Reservoir - a place where fluid collects, especially in rock strata or in the body.

Potassium is a mineral that is found in most foods. Potassium helps to **balance** fluids and minerals in your body. It also helps your body maintain a normal **blood pressure**. Potassium helps your muscles contract and your nerves function normally.

Preventing Goiter. Irritation of the throat area and thyroid gland is known as a "goiter".

Prognosis The outcome of a situation.

Prominence definition of prominence by Medical dictionary. prominence a **protrusion or projection**. frontonasal prominence an expansive facial process in the embryo that develops into the forehead and bridge of the nose; called also frontonasal process.

Resection - the process of cutting out tissue or part of an organ. **"the patient underwent resection of the tumor"**

Spinal Cord Anatomy. The spinal cord is part of the central nervous system (CNS).

Spine a series of vertebrae extending from the skull to the small of the back, enclosing the spinal cord and providing support for the thorax and abdomen; the backbone. "a soft voice that sent a shiver down her spine"

Subcutaneous Passage - Subcutaneous definition is - being, living, occurring, or administered under the skin. How to use **subcutaneous** in a sentence.

Suboccipital mean - medical definition of suboccipital. 1: situated or performed below **the occipital bone**. 2: situated or performed below the occipital lobe of the brain.

Sulcal effacement is a local secondary sign of mass effect in the cranium. Any lesion exerting mass effect on brain parenchyma can push adjacent gyri together, thereby displacing the CSF Cerebos Spinal fluid is a clear, colorless body fluid found in the brain and spinal cord. It is produced by the specialized ependymal cells in the choroid plexuses of the ventricles of the brain, and absorbed in the arachnoid granulations. There is about 125mL of CSF at any one time.

Surgical Surgery simply means **opening the human body and cutting tissues** to treat problems that arise in the body. This may mean removing tissue, altering tissue or simply changing the way the human body works with treatments performed inside the body, typically under anesthesia.

Suture - a stitch or row of stitches holding together the edges of a wound or surgical incision. "sutures are removed on the 5th to 7th day after the operation"

Symptoms A sign is the **effect of a health problem that can be observed by someone else.** A symptom is an effect noticed and experienced only by the person who has the condition. The key difference between signs and symptoms is who observes the effect.

Transitional Meningioma **1.**(*Mesh*)A relatively common neoplasm of the central nervous system that arises from arachnoid AL cells. The majority are well differentiated vascular tumors which grow slowly and have a low potential to be invasive, although malignant subtypes occur. Meningiomas have a predilection to arise from the parasagittal region, cerebral convexity, sphenoidal ridge, olfactory groove, and spinal canal.

Tumor is an **abnormal lump of body tissue**. You can get a tumor if cells grow and copy themselves too fast or don't die when they should. A tumor can be malignant (cancerous) or benign (not cancerous).

Vasogenic cerebral edema. It is an **extracellular edema** which mainly affects the white matter via leakage of fluid from capillaries. It is most frequently seen around brain tumors (both primary and secondary) and cerebral abscesses, though some vasogenic edema may be seen around maturing cerebral contusion and cerebral hemorrhage.

ACKNOWLEDGMENTS AND APPRECIATION

I thank my husband, Joseph, and doctors at the UW Health, for sharing medical information for developing this book. I thank his continued patience and support in helping me be successful as a loving wife and mother of our children. I thank him for allowing me to share my stories especially for continuing to expand my understanding and ability to honor my family. His suggestions and comments have provided better understanding of what I'm writing about.

    I thank my son Aaron and daughter Valerie for their love and guidance and admiration. Being a parent is a joy to diminish the pressures of a busy lifestyle. I thank them for their appreciation of what I do. I also thank my grand-daughter, Valendice for assisting with computer dynamics and skills and creativity and excellence on her part. I thank my sister Helena for distributing business cards and flyers in London to her churchgoers and friends and to try to establish connection to sell/market my books in London bookstores and libraries.

    I thank by brother Denis for purchasing my books in London through Amazon. Now he realizes his little sister can make him smile as he reads her books. I thank my nephew Desmond for providing family deeds and to keep me updated on what is happening on the island.

    I want to thank my nieces, Lina, Gean, and Elaine in London for sending me prayers and videos with songs and music with people dancing from different events in St. Lucia and other islands. This is very much appreciated as those videos keep me up-to-date on how people live in St. Lucia as this helps remembering where I came from immensely.

I want to thank my niece, Kathy for sending me virtual flowers from St. Lucia. This is so amazing as we don't see each other often, but remember there is an aunty in the United States of America. I want to thank Barb for proofing my books and make suggestions to improve my writing skills and style. Her intelligent conversations immensely help the development of this book. I want to thank my nephew, Harry, for sharing his excitement in purchasing my book and entertaining his wife and children.

HOW TO PROTECT YOUR BRAIN

Knowledge is power.

The more you read, the more you feed your brain.
Tips to lower your risk for Alzheimer's and dementia:

- Walk and/or engage in other exercises several times a week to stay active are important lifestyle choices.
- Keep your brain active with crossword puzzles, board games, word search, reading, problem solving, etc.
- Socialize with relative and friends, or volunteer for a no-profit organization.
- Maintain a healthy weight.
- Follow a heart healthy diet.
- Maintain a consistent bed and rise time and limit napping to one time earlier during the day.
- Keep your blood pressure in check.
- Limit alcohol use, and beverages.
- Keep stress and anxiety low.
- Have regular checkups with your doctor.

Alzheimer's is not a normal part of aging. People with memory loss symptoms should be seen by a physician early to determine if there are other factors, including medication side effects or other treatable medical conditions.

There is no cure for Alzheimer's, but research has determined certain medication might pay a role in slowing the progression of some symptoms.

ABOUT THE AUTHOR

PROTECT THE BRAIN WITH MENINGIOMA SURGERY MEMOIR

FIRST EDITION

This author wrote this book after she retired from the State of Wisconsin and the State Lab of Hygiene at the University of Wisconsin. Anne Marie Herman likes to write about herself and achievements. This is the third book she has written.

The author was born on the island of St. Lucia, and her father died very young at the age of 35 and left six children behind for her mother to care. He was a farmer who planted gardens, vegetables, fruits, and raised domesticated animals such as pigs, goats, sheep, horses, cows and chicken. She was the youngest daughter, at only one and a half years old. She has one sister who lives in London, England from the 1960s. Her mother and herself raised three of her sister's children until they were old enough to travel to England and to join their parents.

At age 16, the author cooked more seriously for her oldest brother Jerome, who had lived in London, England for many years and returned to St. Lucia. He died from a heart attack. The author stayed at her brother's house while attending school and went to her mother's house on weekends. Sometimes her brother brought guests to his home for supper, and she would entertain by preparing the meals. Her second oldest brother Robert came back from England and worked as a taxi driver. Neither brothers liked to dine at any restaurants as they were not used to eating food other people cooked and they were not married. As a good Samaritan, the author woke up early and cooked for her brothers before going to work, thus her brothers were assured of getting home cooked meals. Sometimes on Sundays, she would visit her mother and the neighbor would cook for Robert, but he didn't like the cooking. That became a serious problem so she carried some food to him whenever she spent time at her mother's house at the countryside.

The author came to the states to join her husband while he was in the United States military and stationed at Fort Carson, Colorado. They got married in St. Lucia and he left to report back on base for duties. She stayed behind for a short time until she joined her husband in Colorado Springs, Colorado. They had two great children and raised them in Colorado and have since moved to Wisconsin.

When we lived in Colorado, she worked at the Broadmoor Hotel. We realized that I was not familiar or comfortable with my job, as I had previously worked as a private school teacher. With the assistance of the Urban League in Colorado Springs, they talked her in becoming a US citizen and took the oath. Afterwards, she attended the El Paso Community College and earned an Associate in Science degree. In so doing, she worked for the Operations and Maintenance Service (Project Headquarters for the Air Force) and worked in the Purchasing Section for Work Study at the Dean of Instructions Office at the El Paso Community College.

When we came to Madison in 1974, there weren't too many Caribbean foods around the supermarkets or restaurants. We noticed the grocery stores did not carry some authentic food products. My family traveled to Milwaukee to visit my cousin; she took us around to different supermarkets to purchase goods, there were several markets with imported products. By talking to other folks in the area, we discovered some of the grocery stores did carry limited amounts of authentic goods. Some of the produce are called different names in the Caribbean. We called my sister in London, England and she indicated there were many more people born in the Caribbean and that produce was available there.

After the author started working for Rayovac in Madison doing dictation, transcriptions, formatting manuscripts and word processing, tables and thought of writing a book was getting more serious.

She collected recipes from family members and friends by asking what ingredients they used in food to get ideas for a family cookbook and to pass cooking ideas to her children. She also used recipes from former coworkers who brought treats to work and shared their recipes. This book also includes picnics in Madison where people brought treats and shared the ingredients in their recipes. My niece shares cake recipes she bakes as a hobby and business and also makes pastries for her customers. She bakes and decorates cakes for weddings and is very proficient at it. My sister who indicated the drinks people love in England and in St. Lucia when they have gotten together' and parties. Today this looks like a dream come true.

With the help of my husband, my children, grand children, I cook meals based on what they liked especially fish with gravy. I cooked chicken and very small dumplings for my grand children, as this dish is one of their favorite meals.

The author watched the movie "Julia and Julia" many times looking at how a book was created. She has read the book "Will Write for Food by Diane Jacob" which is a Complete Guide to Writing a cookbook, reviews, memoirs, and more. This book gave her a good inspiration on how to describe foods, its taste, and smell. She has also contacted Ms. Jacob for ideas.

The author's son-in-law has indicated that her cooked fish is "the bomb" and have since learned how to cook fish my style to entertain his buddies after sharing my cooking secrets. The author has prepared fish for church gatherings, and the congregation wowed the taste of her cooking. With this said, the author is ready to produce another book.

After her family and kids came to Madison, the author was employed at Rayovac Corporation. She took evening classes while working for the state. She attended Madison Area Technical College and earned a Human Resource Certificate and took various Microsoft Office classes to brush up my computer skills. For two years, she attended Leadership Institute at Work at the UW for professional development. She was a Program Assistant/Office Manager during the time she worked for the state, and was a Site Manager/Financial Specialist at the UW.

Prior to going to the UW, she was involved in Toastmasters of Madison program. This was a learning experience about writing and presented persuasive speeches on a weekly basis. It was a matter of concentrated listening and to critique the speaker from everything that was said during a presentation. That is when she decided to take a class on the Art of Public Speaking at MATC. This gave her techniques on analyzing a speech, how to put a speech together, and to communicate with the audience. In that she stopped worrying, and cut down on nervousness used eye contact and visual aids and did some critical thinking.

My son-in-law has indicated that my cooked fish is "the bomb" and have since learned how to cook fish my style to entertain his buddies after sharing my cooking secrets. I have prepared fish for church gatherings, and the congregation wowed the taste of my cooking.

During the past several years, the author lost four brothers, one from a heart attack and the other from heart failure. Her youngest brother died from liver cancer, and another brother died from prostate cancer. Since living in Madison, the author has lost four brothers and her mother and that's pretty tragic for the rest of the family. The author hope to donate some of the benefits from this book for cancer research. Today this looks like a dream come true.

Also by Anne Marie Herman, Author

Protect the Brain with Meningioma Surgery, Memoir

Anne Marie's Family Favorite Recipes with a
Caribbean Twist 2018 – Second Edition

Positive Affirmation – Fear No More Memoir
Some Suggestions to Reverse Type 2 Diabetes 2020
First Edition

www.ingramcontent.com/pod-product-compliance
Lightning Source LLC
Chambersburg PA
CBHW052116110526
44592CB00013B/1631